Simple RADICAL Prayer

P. Douglas Small

Alive Publications

Simple Radical Prayer

ISBN: 978-0-9975802-8-0

©Copyright 2016 by P. Douglas Small

Published by Alive Publications
a division of
Alive Ministries: PROJECT PRAY
PO Box 1245
Kannapolis, NC 28082

www.alivepublications.org

www.projectpray.org

Scripture quotations, unless otherwise indicated are taken from the Holy Bible, New King James Version, Copyright – 1979, 1980, 1982, 1990, 1995, Thomas Nelson, Inc., Publishers.

Dedication

To Bennie Triplett

My first State Overseer, who believed in Barbara and me and gave us our first opportunity in full-time ministry.

And to the wonderful folks of the Dakotas – so kind and patient in our formative learning years, so many of whom have remained friends for decades.

Contents

1

Not What – Who

Listen, my friend! Your helplessness is your best prayer. It calls from your heart to the heart of God with greater effect than all your uttered pleas. He hears it from the very moment that you are seized with helplessness, and He becomes actively engaged at once in hearing and answering the prayer of your helplessness.

Ole Kristian O. Hallesby

Bennie Triplett appointed me to my first church. I often wonder if he had second thoughts and if he later regretted it. I was not only green with so much to learn, but I was also a slow learner. Over the years, despite my early faltering, he always remained gracious. He is one of the most beloved preachers in the history of the Church of God and a prolific song writer with a rich baritone voice! What a gift. He was reared at the Church of God Home for Children in Sevierville, Tennessee, now known as Smoky Mountain Children's Home.

> *Prayer is not something you do – it is being with someone you know.*

The day the home acquired the first John Deere tractor, he recalls they were all so proud of it and eager to protect it. Some of the boys had never seen a tractor before – at least, not one up close. Until that time, the fields of crops and vegetables used to feed the children at the home had been plowed by two teams of fine mules – Pet and Lou, and Sam and Mike. Now, with the new tractor, things would be done more effectively and efficiently. The mules could rest and so could the boys. There was new machinery. New modern techniques had come to the home! Not so quick, they would soon learn.

On the first outing, the new John Deere tractor became mired axle-deep in mud. Triplett recalled how enormous and powerful the tractor seemed. The two wheels were as tall as he was at the time, being some 10 or 11 years of age. Even so, those powerful wheels were halfway buried in mud. So much for new technology. There was nothing else to do but to haul out the mules. They did.

The mules were hooked to the tractor, but they tugged and strained in vain. The tractor would not budge. Brother Eller, the Superintendent of the home, called for Tommy Pitman, one of more senior boys. Tommy provided regular care for the mules, fed and groomed them. It was Tommy who typically put the harnesses on them, and then after a vigorous workout, he freed them to roam in the big pasture. Tommy knew those mules – better than anyone. He had a special relationship with them. In the end, it was that relationship that determined the critical difference.

> We have seen prayer as something we do; as an exercise, a list we pray over. Prayer may involve interaction with God about people, places and things, but it is not what you *do* as much as who you are *with*. There is certainly nothing wrong with new methods, even prayer methods. In a pragmatic culture, we have reduced ministry to method and made prayer a pragmatic, outcome based, partner to our work.
>
> Characteristically, when our new approaches fail, we readily fall back on old techniques. In the work of the Lord, techniques alone are never our answer. Today, there is a renewed interest in prayer – but the interest is too often as a technique, a means of church-growth, a tool for more effective evangelism, a component in some

strategic process. The solution is rarely found in method alone. Prayer has no inherent power – the power is in God. Prayer is a healthy, dependable, faith-filled, scripture-based, spirit-empowered asking relationship with God. It is the privilege afforded to God's blood-stained, born-again children. It is a covenant benefit available to the bride-partner of Christ, who, in a relationship with Him, is endeavoring to accomplish mission on His behalf. Someone has to know God, in order to know *the ways* of God.

There is power in prayer out of the relationship; power that flows out of the prayer encounter; power that flows from God due to the relationship we have with Him through Christ.

Tommy arrived at the scene and sized up the situation. He checked the harness and tightened the trace chains. He realigned the team of mules and stroked them. And then he confidently talked them into pulling the tractor out of the axle-deep mud. Triplett remembers how the situation changed when Tommy gave the command: "Pet and Lou hit the traces, the doubletree buckled, 'John Deere' and the mud gave forth a moan, and that new tractor popped up out of the muck and mire like a plastic toy."[1]

Prayer is no old technique to solve some modern problem. It is not a power tool to be used to augment a new program. It is relational, both at its heart (knowing the love of God and loving Him) and at its edge (loving others into His Kingdom, into a relationship with Him). Somebody has to know God, and have a love-empowered, worshipful bond with Him. Prayer calls up power, not because prayer is powerful, but because God is powerful, and a relationship exists that engages Him, as Father, through Christ. Without that relationship, there is no release of power. In truth, it is

---

1   Bennie S. Triplett, *Praying Effectively* (Cleveland, TN: Pathway Press, 1990), 77-78.

not prayer that has power – it has none at all. It is God that has power.

A Covenant Relationship

Christian prayer is an exceptional privilege and its nature is extremely unique among religions. Muslim prayer is distinctly different from Christian prayer, as are Hindu and Buddhist prayer, not to mention pagan prayer models. God has designed prayer as the communication system specifically for those *in a covenant relationship* with Him.[2] Both testaments, old and new, are records of God's revelation, His revealing Himself to man. A testament is a covenant. So the Bible is a record of the covenant God offers man. God has a will – a plan for man. A 'will' is empowered only after the death of its maker, the testator! We have an older will, called the Old Testament, based on the blood of bulls and goats. And we have a new will, called the New Testament. That last will and testament, offered to us by Jesus Christ, was placed into force when he died (Heb. 9:16-17). His shed blood made our relationship with the Father possible (Eph. 2:13). The New Testament, God's last will, the latest and clearest declaration of Christ's desires for us, details prom-

> *Effective prayer is the fruit of a relationship with God, not a technique for acquiring blessings.*
>
> D.A. Carson

---

2   This message is taken from: P. Douglas Small *Transformation Themes*, Chapter Seven, *Prayer,* (Alive Ministries: Kannapolis, NC; May, 2001), 76-87. Published and copyrighted material.

ises to us and the ethical principles incumbent on us, his bride, as his representative people (Mt. 5).

The environment in which God distributes gifts, things from his covenant store to us, revelation and insight, practical and material benefits, is prayer – God speaking to man and man speaking to God. God wants us to know him and to converse with him (James 4:2; John 16:24). He isn't hiding. The interactions of God with man throughout history are found in Scripture. The Bible is essentially a record of these covenants of God with mankind, through Adam and subsequently Noah. And then we have the covenant with Israel through Abraham, Moses and then David. All those have mankind in view and look to the new covenant through Jesus Christ. With each disclosure, the relationship grows. Each covenant is built on the previous one – the covenant with Adam, with Noah, with Abraham, that given through Moses, with David and then the new covenant through the blood of Jesus Christ. Each expands on the previous.

We have seen prayer primarily as "asking" things of God. And certainly, making requests of God is an extraordinary privilege. But it is possible only because of our *relationship* with Him, through Christ (John 10:7; Mt. 11:2:3). The *terms* of our relationship are defined in the Bible – the Old and New Testaments.

A covenant and a contract, at least from a Biblical perspective, are slightly different. A contract is largely consumed with the exchange of goods and services. If one party fails in the exchange of a payment or promises, the contract has been violated and may be broken. In a contract, cost containment and expeditious delivery of goods and services are the great concern.

A covenant, on the other hand, is not primarily about the exchange of goods and services. Rather, it is about the exchange of *persons*. This is the nature of relationship with God, in Christ. He gave us life in Creation. He redeemed us after the fall, in Christ. He made us members of His family. Prayer is the communicative system in this dynamic relationship. The manager of a contract relationship may ask, "How can I get XYZ Company to do what I want them to do, what is best for me and my company, for less money and less bother?" That is the nature of a contract – it is business. And if another company can perform the services better, more efficiently, and with a cost savings, the contract is awarded to that company. That cannot describe our relationship with God. Do we switch gods when we find one who performs for us more effectively or efficiently?

It should be clear that a man asking essentially the same question about his wife would be utterly inappropriate. It would be a sign that the marriage was not healthy. The nature of the love bond in such a marriage is conditional, utilitarian. A marriage may have contractual implications, but the essence of the marriage, like our relationship with God, is more covenant than contract. Any exchange of goods and services is secondary to the relationship itself. Not so with a contract. If a man has a company and a supplier who can't deliver, he finds a vendor who can provide the supplies, no matter how much he likes the previous contractor. But, we don't switch marital partners, and we don't switch gods. Those relationships are not merely contractual in nature. They are covenants – "for better or worse, richer or poorer."

Right Promises and Right Hearts

In one of the more stunning moments in the life of Jesus, he was approached by a Gentile woman who cried out first after Jesus, then after his disciples. She was desperate. But Jesus was unmoved. He displayed no typical compassion. In fact, he seemed uncharacteristically harsh. *"I was not sent except to the lost sheep of the house of Israel"* (Mt. 15:24). Bluntly, she was *outside* the perimeters of *the covenant* provisions, and he would not hear her prayer. He did eventually minister to her, but only when she acknowledged that she did not possess the *rights* she had implied. She had falsely represented herself as being entitled by the use of coded language, *"Son of David"* (Mt. 15:22). After she exhibited pure sincerity and honesty, Jesus responded positively to her. And only when she acknowledged that she was a Gentile, outside the covenant. And then, it was to her pressing claim, that even Gentiles should receive some benefit from the covenant table, that Jesus responded positively (Mt. 15:25-28). It was not an appeal to covenant rights, but to grace and mercy. To that God responds. Only believers, inside the covenant, have the authority and standing to appeal directly to the covenant. So often, we fail to do so. We fail to allow the Scripture to inform our prayer content.

The difference between praying and wishing is simple. Praying interacts with the covenant promises of God and submits to the purposes of that covenant – that all things reveal and glorify God, furthering his kingdom purposes. People who pray over an open Bible are demonstrating evidence of their faith in the covenant. They pray 'right' promises. The people whose prayers are wishful personal fancies, pray differently than those who wrestle in prayer for God's Kingdom to break into the earth, for His will to be enforced, for His heart's desire to become our heart's desire. The latter group prays out of the long covenant history of men and women who sought God's heart for their generation.

The Bible, our covenant with God, is both the catalyst and the context for personal transformation. Prayer is the primary evidence of how vitally alive both our personal and corporate faith really are. There is a difference between a plea for grace and mercy and serious appeal to know the will of God in a particular situation. To be changed, indeed, to grow in grace, requires wrestling our will into alignment with God's will. That happens most naturally over an open Bible or in the light of fresh insight from the Holy Spirit. Sadly, such an idea seems rare among Christians today.

Right Faith in an Unfailing God

In Luke 18 Jesus spoke a parable about praying saying, *"that men always ought to pray and not lose heart"* or not faint. We are not "to not give up" on prayer. The first thing we seem to give up on is prayer! Before we stop attending worship gatherings or church activities, before we cease to listen to gospel singing or preaching, before we end evangelism efforts and Christian education – we give up on prayer. It is always the first step to apostasy. The message that Jesus wants us to take away from this parable is – don't give up on prayer! Paul exhorted the Colossians in the same manner, *"Continue in prayer!"* (Col. 4:2).

The parable in Luke 18 involves a judge. He was not a religious man nor was he a sensitive man. He *"did not fear God nor regard man"* (Luke 18:2). He should not have been a judge. But he was. Before him came a woman. She was twice disadvantaged – she was a female in a man's world and she was a widow. Both rendered her culturally and legally powerless. If she had chosen to remarry, she would have gained the protection of a new husband. But she sought a standing on her own. The idea itself was staggering.

A woman in the first century passed from the control of her father to her husband, usually while still in her teens. She, apart from father or husband, was virtually without property or rights. All assets or rights were usually through a husband. A woman may have shared the wealth of a husband while he was alive, but when that husband died, a widow was at the mercy of her sons or her husband's brothers. They inherited the wealth. Her independent rights were virtually non-existent. A husband's land rights stayed with his family or passed to his sons. Incredibly his widow, stripped of inheritance rights, might be responsible for any of his debts. A widow was classed as a landless stranger – essentially the status of an immigrant.[3]

> *Asking with shameless persistence, the importunity that will not be denied, returns with the answer in hand.*

This bold widow dared to appear before the Judge. She had an adversary who was creating havoc in her life, just as we do in our nemesis, Satan. She pleaded for "justice" from

---

3   www.biblestudytools.com/Dictionairies/BakersEvangelicalDictionary/
     bed.cgi?number=T732. See Widow, Baker Dictionary.

her adversary. It wasn't grace for which she pleaded, or even mercy. She only wanted what was due and fair to any human, justice.

Despite the obvious oppression and the bitter state of her life, the hard-hearted, insensitive judge would not intervene, at least for a while. But she was not easily dissuaded. She was persistent. She was relentless. She would not be intimidated by the resistance of the court. In every way and on a repeated basis, she brought her matter before the judge. Finally, overwhelmed by her resolve, he said within himself, *"Though I do not fear God nor regard man, yet because this widow troubles me I will avenge her, lest by her continual coming she weary me."* With her sheer persistence, she moved this recalcitrant, hard-hearted judge to declare relief for her. Persistence won and she prevailed.

This is a parable of *contrast*. In the story, we are *compared* to the widow and God to the unjust judge. But this is a parable of superficial comparison and profound contrast. Like the widow, we make an appeal to God, the Judge, with the power to decree and launch interventions. But the power of the story is in the double contrast, not the comparison.

Jesus notes, *"Hear what the unjust judge said."* Now the contrast: *"Shall God not avenge His own elect who cry out day and night to Him?...He will avenge them speedily."* First, God is not unjust, and on this point, we find great contrast. There is a huge difference between our prayer to a gracious God, and the widow's appeal to this hard-hearted judge. And there is a second contrast. We, the church, the corporate body of believers, are not a widow. Sadly, the world sees God as belonging to a class of religious founders – all dead. They treat the Resurrection as a metaphor. That makes the Christian faith a set of noble principles taught by a valiant, but dead leader. Christianity involves principles, but it is essentially a relationship. You can recall the memory of a person, and borrow life principles, but to have a relationship with a person demands that they are alive.

Jesus is alive. He isn't dead. The Holy Spirit has been sent as Jesus requested of the Father, as proof of his victory over death and the grave. The Holy Spirit now operates in his name, out of his office, in the church to simulate his life and finish his mission. We are 'the bride,' the elect, the chosen of God. And our bridegroom, though presumed dead by the world, is very much alive. He is enthroned on David's throne, not in Jerusalem, but in heaven. He is the last Adam, the King of the earth and he is now reigning in exile, until his bride partner completes her mission.

The text instructs us: When heaven does not respond, don't draw harsh conclusions about God. Persist in prayer. Don't give up. And second, by inference, remember your standing as the 'bride-partner' of the living Christ, raised from the dead. What could be impossible for him? What prayer could he not answer? Refuse, as did this widow, to see yourself as powerless. In fact, God delights to answer prayer in the name of Jesus as proof that Jesus is not dead, but alive.

"Nevertheless, when the Son of Man comes, will He really find faith on the earth?" In the middle of verse 8, there is a dramatic turn. The question posed by Jesus seems utterly out of place. What possible connection could this eschatological question have to do with this parable? It may be the most profound insight of all. Very simply, the survival of faith on the earth is rooted in persistent prayer. Not in open

churches or an underground movement due to persecution. Not in the operation of our Christian colleges, our seminaries or other Christian enterprise operations – but simply in a praying bride.

Discussion Questions

1. Hallesby says, "Your helplessness is your best prayer." Have you ever felt helpless as you prayed? Did you feel such a prayer was effective? Faithless? Talk about it.

2. We have seen prayer as something we do, as an exercise, a list we pray over. In a pragmatic culture, we have reduced ministry to method and made prayer a pragmatic, outcome-based partner to our work. Is prayer an exercise, a list – answered by pragmatic outcomes?

3. Prayer has no inherent power – the power is in God. Do you agree or disagree?

4. Talk about the difference between a covenant and a contract. How does that relate to prayer?

5. What is the difference between wishing and praying?

2

Prayer as Mystery

Our ordinary views of prayer are not found in the New Testament. We look upon prayer as a means for getting something for ourselves; the Bible idea of prayer is that we may get to know God Himself.

Oswald Chambers

In a "science-soaked" culture, prayer is something we struggle to comprehend. We see it as pragmatic and want to understand its "workings" rather than rest in the relationship itself. Einstein is said to have been asked near the end of his life if there were other arenas that he would have liked to have pursued, other mysteries that he would like to have unraveled. Einstein's response was simply that someone needed to "check out prayer!" There is a power attached to prayer. Power that dances in and around prayer. And yet it cannot be understood in a mere cause-effect manner. The power is not prayer's power, it is God's power. Prayer is mystery, because God is mysterious. So, prayer doesn't collaborate well with science. It is essentially relational. It is an interaction between unpredictable people and an utterly reliable, but mystifying God. Depend on Him, but don't dictate His course of action. Bank on His provision, but don't calculate His ways and means so as to reduce Him to a puppet. Count on an answer, but be prepared for one different than you might have anticipated. He demands His role as God. He is not interested in switching positions with us as the lords, with Him as servant. Prayer is not a bell that he answers. Richard Foster believes,

> Our problem is that we assume prayer is something to master the way we master algebra or auto mechanics. That puts us in the "on top" position, where we are competent and in control. But when praying, we come "underneath" where we calmly and deliberately surrender the control and become incompetent...the truth of the matter is, we all come to prayer with a tangled mass of motives altruistic and selfish, merciful and hateful, loving and bitter. Frankly, this side of eternity we will never unravel the good from the bad, the pure from the impure. God is big enough to receive us with all our mixture. That is what grace means, and not only are we saved by it, we live by it as well. And we pray by it.[4]

Prayer is perplexing, because it is tied to the heart of a God whose ways are past finding out, whose foolishness is beyond our collective human wisdom. Grace, not technique, makes our prayer life successful. God's goodness, not our good praying, is the driving force behind prayer's answers (Mt. 7:11; James 1:17). And yet, prayer is the very process by which He changes and alters us.

A Culture that is Not a Praying Culture

Perhaps, in part, because of our cultural baptism in pragmatism and predictable outcomes, we have drifted from prayer. Whatever the reason, it is clear now that we are not a praying culture. The Hindu culture is a praying culture. The Buddhist culture is a praying culture. If you travel to the Middle East and are in any Muslim area when the call to prayer is given, you will watch grown, strong men fall to their knees, bow their faces to the ground and pray to Allah.

---

4   Richard J. Foster *Prayer: Finding the Heart's True Home* (New York: Harper-Collins, 1992), 7.

The same is true of Jews. On any El AL flight to Jerusalem, Orthodox Jews will crowd to the eastern end of the jet come sunrise for a time of prayer. With a prayer book in hand and a talit over their head, they will pray openly in the aisle of the plane. No shame. No dishonor. No reticence. They will stand openly at the Wailing Wall in Jerusalem and wail! Majority World Christian cultures are full of praying people.

> *It is a tremendously hard thing to pray aright, yea, it is verily the science of all sciences.*
>
> *Martin Luther*

America is not a praying culture. It has increasingly become an anti-prayer culture. We have allowed a legal war on public prayer to prevail in our nation. We continue to systematically remove all public liberty in the area of prayer, particularly Christian prayer, specifically prayer in the name of Jesus. Samuel Chadwick believed prayer should be pervasive, "There is nothing about which I do not pray. I go over all my life in the presence of God. All my problems are solved there."[5]

Churches that Do Not Pray

Not only is America not a praying culture, but America's church is not a praying church. The average American church member prays four minutes a day. And most of that, I jokingly add, is for a parking place near the door at the neighborhood Wal-Mart. A survey taken in a church in Alberta, Canada asked this question: What kind of prayer life

---

5   Samuel Chadwick, *The Path of Prayer*, 100.

do you have? Are you a crisis pray-er? A casual pray-er? Or a committed pray-er? Of 300 responses, 276 classified themselves as crisis or casual pray-ers. Only 24 or 8 percent met the criteria of being a committed person of prayer.

The theology books of the 1970's and 1980's almost never mention prayer, at least in a direct way. Prayer has been ignored by our culture and ignored by the North American Church. Until a few years ago, only one American seminary taught a class on prayer. Most Bible colleges and seminaries do not even classify prayer as a theological item. It is seen, if at all, as a mere component of discipleship or Christian Ministries.

A survey of 572 United States pastors demonstrated that 57 percent prayed less than 20 minutes a day. That means that the total time spent in prayer, in communion and consultation with God by American pastors, is just over two hours per week. Another 34 percent of American pastors pray for 20 minutes or more per day, but less than an hour per day. The average time spent in prayer by American pastors is 22 minutes per day – 2.5 hours per week. An average of 22 minutes a day for those who are the spiritual guides of the faithful and the leaders of moral renewal for the nation. In Australia the average is 23 minutes. In New Zealand, it is 30 minutes. In Japan, hardly a Christian nation, it is a surprising 44 minutes and in Korea, it is 90 minutes a day.[6]

A Practice So Little Understood

Why do we ignore prayer? It seems that prayer is so contrary to our utilitarian, pragmatic way of approaching life

---

6   Study by Peter Wagner.

in America. We are an action-oriented culture. Our sports and entertainment options demand excitement. Television turns a scene every few seconds. Lifetimes are collapsed into short reviews. Complex mysteries are solved in an hour with time for dramatic commercials. In comparison, we may see no immediate and measurable results from private and quiet seasons of prayer. So we conclude that it is a nice thing, a noble thing, a sweet thing – but not a fundamentally essential thing. That is not what Scripture indicates. It is something we all know deep in our hearts, but the effect of the world's pace on our hectic lives and its clouding of Biblical thinking renders us increasingly prayerless.

Prayer, it turns out, is the consistently untested and untried element in our American ministries. We bake our spiritual cakes without it and the taste seems the same. It isn't the same! The problem is our almost complete loss of discernment. We think of prayer as optional, like we think about the human appendix or the tonsils. You can live with them or without them, and life seems to go on just the same – maybe better. At any rate, we treat prayer like an inessential. A pastor told me recently, "I had never considered prayer that important until I heard you passionately talk about it." This Pentecostal pastor admitted that he needed to go home and reconsider the importance of prayer. Incredible! The Scripture considers prayer to be indispensable. If spirit is breath to us, then prayer is breathing. There is no life in the body of Christ without it. No true life!

It is true that prayer is somewhat of a mystery. We pray, and nothing seems to happen. Then things happen that cannot be traced to any specific prayer. That mystifies us. We make a particular request of God in prayer, and instead of getting what we had asked for, we get something completely different. At times, it is something wonderful, something that we would have never dared to ask of God. We get the unstated desire of our hearts. At other times, the answer seems to disappoint us – at least for a season. Then one day, we have an *"aha!"* moment. Looking back, we realize that if we had gotten what we had requested, it would not have been in our best interest. Instead, our path took a different turn. It was a confusing season at first, disappointing to us in an acute way, but in time we see the truth of Romans 8:28. God was working in our lives in ways that we could not have understood then, even if an angel had been sent to have coffee with us and explain God's plan.

> Our faith may be resting on a wrong basis: faith in faith or faith in prayer rather than faith in God.
>
> — Ivan French

Prayer is not about directing God. It is not about moving his hand. Requests and petitions are legitimate components of prayer. Desire for counsel and wisdom, for direction and clarity are sometimes what drive us into encounters with God in prayer. But prayer is not exchanging information with God. Or printing out the directions for our lives for the next day or week. It is not a Christian's substitute for a horoscope.

A Relational Perspective Ignored

Like the covenant, prayer is relational. It is not a conversation over the details of a contract. It is not a dispute over mere stuff. It is the affirmation of our trust in God and His word. It is a celebration of our faith, an action that says daily, by the investment our time, that He is involved in our lives even if in sometimes invisible and undetectable ways. It is the tender evidence that we believe in His love and grace. The power is not in our words, rather, it is when something deep inside of us touches something deep inside of God – and we know that we know that He is there. The power is in God – His Presence and disclosures. Trust, in such moments, is complete. And in such moments, we are certain everything will be all right. Such occasions defy words. They cannot always be translated conceptually or expressed verbally.

However, this is not a mere "feeling" that we are describing. It is more than emotion. It is spiritual. It has a texture beyond emotion. It has life about it. Life that is bigger than we can produce in and of ourselves. We have entered in such moments into the arena of God's presence by the mystery of prayer and we are sensing His power and presence. We are not so much as moving His hand as we are placing ourselves in His hand.

A Transformational Dynamic that is Resisted

Prayer is the context in which we honor and sustain our covenantal relationship with God. E. Stanley Jones said:

> In prayer you align yourself to the purpose and power of God and His is able to do things through you that you could not otherwise do...for this is an open universe, where some things are left open, contingent upon our doing them...and they will never be done except as we pray.[7]

---

7   Cheri Fuller, *The One Year Praying Through the Bible*. (Tyndale House Publishers, 2013), 14.

That is a fascinating quote. Jones argues that prayer is an "aligning" experience. Something imperceptible happens to us as we pray. It is not God that is changed by our prayer or moved by it. We are moved. And we are strangely moved in a way that reorders us, bringing us under His sovereign custody. Without this alignment, this change in us and our relationship with God by the process of prayer, there are things that God could not and would not do through us. Of course, it is not God that is limited by our lack of prayer. We are limited in terms of participation in His work.

Jones goes so far as to argue that "some things will never be done except as we pray." He offers us the idea of an "open" universe, a concept that suggest that the sovereign God has left some ends to our discretion and yet simultaneously subordinate to participation with Him in prayer. He could but He will not. Mysteriously, He has yielded some things to the persistence of man through the discipline of prayer. It turns out, "God governs the world by prayer!"

Prayer – The Essential for Appropriations from God

Andrew Murray says,

> God's intense longing to bless seems to be graciously limited by His dependence upon intercession...God regards intercession as the highest expression of His people's readiness to receive and yield themselves wholly to the working of His almighty power.[8]

In a similar vein, Andrew Murray asserts that the bless-

---

8   Andrew Murray, *God's Best Secrets: An Inspirational Daily Devotional* (Grand Rapids: MI; Kregel Publications, 1993), 45.

ings of God themselves are accessed only through prayer, 'graciously limited' by God's use of prayer. James, the brother of Jesus agrees, *"You have not, because ye ask not!"* (James 4:2).

But again, prayer is not a mere *means* of "withdrawing grace" from the believer's heavenly account. James warns that prayer stubbornly yields blessings if we utilize it to "consume" it upon our lusts. And Murray notes that the response of God in blessing is not merely to prayer itself, but to what is happening to us and in us by the experience of prayer. Intercession is an *expression* of our *readiness* to *receive* and *yield*. Here is the idea of alignment again, expressed in a different way. Murray observes that all of this is happening in order that we might be available to be used of God, to participate wholly in the working of God's almighty power.

Prayer is the context in which God changes us in order that He might work in us and through us to accomplish His purposes and fulfill our destiny. The power is found in the way that prayer transforms us and makes us available to be used of God. Its efficacy is not in well-formed phrases. It is not our impressive grasp of theology expressed heavenward. It is not inspiring liturgy. The power and effectiveness out of prayer is in something deeper. It is not our strength in prayer but our weakness openly declared before our Father, God. It is the place when we at the end, our self, our own resources and solutions, wrap ourself in faith and hope, put our trust in His character and cry out to God. That is when prayer is most effective.

Discussion Questions

1. How does the science-soaked culture of our day impact faith in prayer?

2. Richard Foster says, "We don't master prayer, if it is not a technique." Read his quote on page 22 and discuss it.

3. Why is there a war on prayer in our culture?

4. If prayer is about directing God or moving His hand – what is prayer?

5. Discuss prayer as an alignment (see the quote by E. Stanley Jones on pages 29-30).

3

Prayer as Purifying

What is the reason that some believers are so much brighter and holier than others? I believe the difference in nineteen cases out of twenty, arises from different habits about private prayer. I believe that those who are not eminently holy pray little and those who are eminently holy pray much.

James Charles Ryle

On the bumper of the car was a fish sticker – a Christian symbol. And in the symbol, was the word "Jesus." Here was a born-again, "Jesus"-loving kind of Christian. On the other side of the car's bumper was another sticker, a dove. Ah, a Spirit-filled Christian. On the back window was the decal of a Christian college. So, my friend reasoned, here was a born-again, Spirit-filled believer, who had attended a Christian college. He could be a preacher! Getting even closer, my friend saw that there was an air-freshener hanging from the rear-view mirror. Unbelievable. Unreal. Puzzling. It was the silhouette of a Playboy bunny.

Winston Churchill once declared that England needed "a supreme recovery of moral health and martial vigor." America now seems to be in the same place, lacking in both moral clarity of values and force of character. Dr. Erwin W. Lutzer, Senior Pastor of Chicago's Moody Church observed that the evangelical ship is taking on water. He cautions, "The church cannot be inundated by worldly values and yet meet its responsibility of keeping society from decay. If our assignment is to reclaim the moral ground of this nation for righteousness, how can we do it if we ourselves are guilty of the same sins?" Only if we are "brought to our knees, God may begin to give us spiritual victories that could stem abortion, infanticide and drug abuse...The greatest need for the church today is believing prayer."

Over 90 percent of American's say that they pray, at least on some occasions. But less than 50 percent in any region of the United States, including the deeply religious south and the conservative mid-west, pray about the moral choices they make in life. We have developed a kind of wall of separation between the help we ask of God, and the foul lines of morality. Prayer should be a purifying experience. Talking to and fellowshipping with a holy God should change us. Charles Spurgeon declared, "God visits every house where night and morning prayers are made, but where these are neglected, sin is incurred."[9] Spurgeon's thesis notes that prayer makes hearts and homes holy.

Here are the concerns.

1. We Have Re-Created God and Re-Fashioned Faith

---

9   Mary Ann Bridgwater, Beth Moore, Jerry Rankin, *Prayers for the Faithful: Fervent Daily Prayer and Meditations* (B and H Publishing Group: Nashville, TN; 2008), 428.

We seem to have developed for ourselves a "nurturing faith" that is too often detached from the concept of God's holiness and our sinful condition. In effect, we have recreated God, or attempted to do so. We have fixed in our minds the limiting image and perception of Him as helper. He *is* a "very present" help in trouble (Psalm 46:10). Indeed, we are told, *"Call upon the Lord in the time of trouble"* and he would deliver (Psalm 50:15; 86:7).

Such deliverance provides the opportunity for us to glorify Him (Psa. 50:15). But that requires us to be a credible witness. In the day of Jeremiah, the Lord instructed him to inform the people that God would not hear (Jeremiah 11:14), and that his refusal was traceable to their moral and spiritual rebellion. They had disqualified themselves as witnesses in God's behalf. Such a message was no more popular then than it is now. Jeremiah was censored and placed in prison for his blunt and politically incorrect speech.

Our culture wants love, but often without truth. We are open to his affirmation, but resistant to conviction, to moral transformation. This notion of a "nurturing faith" which does not demand lifestyle change or moral-purity with personal discipline is immensely popular, if not pervasive, in the church today. But it is not a Biblical notion at all. Biblical prayer is transformational. Love constrains. It does not offer a lower standard than the law, but one that is higher (Mt. 5:17-20). Our righteousness must exceed that of the Scribes and Pharisees. We are called to adopt the model of the Father – to grow toward maturity, to be whole, healthy, "perfect" like the Father (Mt. 5:48).

The nature of our covenant with God is not merely to allow us to access grace, as if it were a free divine ATM card to be used recklessly. And here is the mystery – grace is free. And it is unlimited. And it is lavishly applied to sinful hearts. And yet, grace is not cheap. Nor is it the ultimate gift God wants to give us. Grace is an empowering means to a greater end. God wants us to be like His son, Jesus. Grace is both space and energy. First, it is the relational space in which a holy God works with and in sinners. It is the arena in which he transforms sinners into saints. Second, grace is also the energy that drives the transforming process, by which he changes us to Christ-like sons and daughters, and then uses us in mission. Grace is free to us. On the other hand, it is heaven's costliest investment. And our choice to not waste such a lavish gift is evidence of our awareness of His nature.

2. We see Prayer as Transaction – Not as a Transformation

Prayer cannot be perceived as merely "doing business" with God. It is not primarily *transactional*. Again, it is *transformation*. *We* seek the *hand* of God. We want that divine hand to perform in our behalf. God seeks to place us in *His hand.* He longs for us to seek "His face." For in seeing His face, we are moved at the very core of our being. An encounter with the sovereign God of Scripture will not and cannot leave you and me the same.

Here is the idea of *incarnation*. God seeks to change us in order that He might be revealed *in* us and *through* us. A part of that transformation is the impartation of His holiness and our resultant sensitivity to purity. Prayer should be a purifying experience.

3. We Need a Humbling Encounter

The Scripture says: *"Submit yourselves therefore to God. Resist the devil, and he will flee from you"* (James 4:6).

There is no place where we more clearly submit to God following the master's example than in prayer – *"Not my will, but your will be done!"* Notice that *"resistance"* to the devil and *"submission"* to God are parallel processes. Our capacity to resist in an overcoming way is connected to our submission. Satan flees not due to the personal force of our resistance, but due to the level of our submission! It is not us that he fears. It is the One to whom we are submitted. He would devour us, but we are under the shadow of the One whose mere breath will destroy him (2 Thess. 2:8). Lone rangers who pretend to be spiritual Rambos may go about the country wielding their personal spiritual power, screaming at the darkness, but it is the quiet and humble servant that is the most effective slayer of the dragon. The Devil runs from such saints – behind them is God, terrible and awesome.

> *Prayer will promote our personal holiness as nothing else, except the study of the Word of God.*

Imagine an enemy, spotting a victim, his prey, and closing in for the kill. Suddenly the victim bends downward and bows toward the ground. To the predator, it is unclear what his actions mean or what his intent might be. Momentarily, there is a pause in the action. And then, revealed behind the supposed victim is the predator's own nemesis, his most deadly enemy. Suddenly, the battle shifts. The hunter is now threatened. He has pursued his victim only to run blindly into a trap, face-to-face, with his own worst enemy. His only option is retreat. He must flee. We *"submit to God"* and *"resist the Devil"* and he flees. Not by our power, but because of the One who is always with us. *"Humble yourselves in the sight of the Lord, and he shall lift you up"* (James 4:10).

Exaltation comes from God. And humility is the condition that allows God to raise us up. Pride brings the resistance of God. But humility is the requisite for being given trust by God. No clearer role is there for prayer than that of humbling us!

4. We Need a Purifying Experience

Augustine prayed,

> Breathe in me, O Holy Spirit, that my thoughts may all be holy. Act in me, O Holy Spirit, that my work, too, may be holy. Draw my heart, O Holy Spirit, that I love but what is holy. Strengthen me, O Holy Spirit, to defend all that is holy. Guard me, then, O Holy Spirit, that I always may be holy.[10]

Augustine believed prayer challenged and changed our thought-life. It impacts our actions. It sanctifies our work. It redirects our affections. It infuses us with divine might. It makes us vigilant defenders of the sacred. And it invites God, the Holy Spirit, to hedge us in, that we might fulfill God's purposes in a worthy manner. *"Draw nigh to God, and he will draw nigh to you. Cleanse your hands, ye sinners; and*

---

10   Carolyn Thomas, *Reading the Letters of Saint Paul* (Paulist Press, 2002), 89.

purify your hearts, ye double minded" (James 4:8).

The experience of prayer – *"draw near to God"* – is again referenced. We demonstrate the discipline of prayer by coming near to Him by prayer. And when we do, He comes near to us! Such a process, James declares, results in other changes. When God comes near – hands must be cleansed. If we are to touch Him, it must be with holy hands. If we are to handle holy things, our hands must be sanctified. If the people we touch are not to be contaminated, we must touch them in holy ways with pure hands. In the Old Testament, unwashed hands conferred no blessing – even if a blessing was pronounced. The words of a man's mouth and the actions of his hands are bound together.When God comes near – hands and hearts must be pure. God discerns the things that are hidden to others. An impure heart is the source of a double mind. The heart controls the head. Indecision is rooted in a polluted heart. An unchanged heart is one that has not been challenged by the presence of God in prayer. Transformational prayer.

Remember, in the tabernacle, there were two prayer altars. The first dealt with sin. It invited the sinner. Beyond it was the laver of cleansing, consecration, and beyond, a second altar of Incense. It was the altar of intercession and communion.

5. We Need an Integrity Builder

"Confess your faults one to another, and pray one for another, that ye may be healed" (James 5:16).

Rarely do most churches experience an authentic confessional environment. We may move through a liturgy of confession and offer one another the blessing of peace, but we rarely experience the tear-stained, heart-felt, humbling, and unifying confessional environment that is in view here. And the context is that of prayer. Here is genuine openness and transparent honesty. Here, with our flaws unhidden, yet not flaunted, we are in pursuit of God and His healing hand.

The whole church wants to be healed, and it must realize that something is preventing that wholeness. It cannot be merely the physical that James has in mind here. There is more. Prayer creates an atmosphere that encourages candor with trust, vulnerability and personal growth. In prayer, I see myself as undone (Isa. 6), and I simultaneously long to be healed. It is in this prayerful environment that healing power is released. In this environment, honesty is exhibited before God and one another, and then wrapped in prayer. And the power of God comes.

Ole Hallesby believed,

> When we go to our meeting with God, we should go like a patient to his doctor, first to be thoroughly examined and afterwards to be treated for our ailment. Then something will happen when you pray.[11]

We have people today who want to be healed, but they will not allow themselves to come into a place of open and honest self-examination. They compartmentalize themselves, offering God their body for repair, but keeping the soul and the spirit out of the process. This is not the typical prayer request that James has in view. More is being exchanged here, than the presenting issue. This is not confession of mere physical maladies or aches and pains. This

---

11   Ole Hallesby, *Prayer* (Minneapolis: MN: Augsburg Publishing House, 1931; Augsburg Fortress, 1994), 97.

is a confession of faults. The Greek word is *paraptoma*, (par-ap'-to-mah). It means a side-slip, a lapse or deviation whether it was unintentional error or willful transgression. It can also mean a fall – as in a moral fall, some character fault, some persistent offense, or it may mean sin or trespass. This is not what we typically confess to one another.

In fact, discretion and social training encourage us to "hide such things." Pride demands that we do so. But in prayer – in the moments when we meet Divine Holiness – we are moved into disclosure. Suddenly, the context of corporate prayer becomes confessional. In honesty before God, coupled with brokenness and prayer one for another, the power of God is released to begin to heal us.

Why are there so many sick among us? Why do we not see healing power? Is the day of miracles over? Is it a lack of faith? Perhaps it is because we want healing but we do not want the humility required to confess our faults, the shame of the public admission that we are not all we appear to be. *"Confess your faults one to another, and pray one for another, that ye may be healed"* (James 5:16). Bound by our pride, we retain the hidden sin of our hearts. We remain tight-lipped and we consequently seal our-

> *Walking with God down the avenue of prayer we acquire something of His likeness, and unconsciously we become witnesses to others of His beauty and His grace.*
>
> — E. M. Bounds

selves off from the healing power of God. Great revivals involved the open confession of sin, not merely miracles.

6. We Need the Power of Righteousness

"The effectual fervent prayer of a righteous man availeth much" (James 5:16). This scripture says it is the energized prayer – the effectually fervent prayer – of a righteous man that is effective. Prayer is the environment that keeps us practically righteous. And it demands our sensitivity to righteousness or it is a futile exercise.

The Psalmist declared: *"If I regard iniquity in my heart, the Lord will not hear me"* (Psalm 66:18).

Iniquity. Here is another command for purity and righteousness. The Hebrew word for "regarding" iniquity is *ra'ah,* (raw-aw') which means to see or to recognize. It may also mean to approve of, to behold in an admiring way. It can even mean to enjoy. God is saying, "If you can see iniquity inside yourself, don't expect me to hear you." Or, "If you are going to talk with me, you have to put that away. I will not allow you to experience iniquity, or gaze at it, or enjoy it in any way, and talk with me simultaneously." God insists that I must respect His holiness. There is to be a reverence for and of His purity that impacts me. Changes me.

In one of the most frequently quoted passages of the Old Testament we hear:

> *If my people, which are called by my name, shall humble themselves, and pray, and seek my face, and turn from their wicked ways; then will I hear from heaven, and will forgive their sin, and will heal their land.* (2 Chronicles 7:14).

The Septuagint substitutes the word repent for humble.

A nation changes because it honors God's name. It is humble enough to repent before His holiness. It prays – really prays. It seems more than God's hand of blessing, it seeks the approval of His smiling face. And it turns, it changes course, from its wicked ways.

J. C. Ryle asked:

> What is the reason that some believers are so much brighter and holier than others? I believe the difference in nineteen cases out of twenty, arises from different habits about private prayer. I believe that those who are not eminently holy pray little and those who are eminently holy pray much.[12]

Jerry Bridges noted:

> Many Christians have what we might call a "cultural holiness". They adapt to the character and behavior pattern of Christians around them. As the Christian culture around them is more or less holy, so these Christians are more or less holy. But God has not called us to be like those around us. He has called us to be like himself. Holiness is nothing less than conformity to the character of God.[13]

Let's review. Sumbit to God; resist the Devil. Choose God's side. Surrender. Fight the evil desire. Humble yourself – the battle is too big for you. Draw near to God – move closer. Change your behaviors if they are contaminating. Keep a pure heart. Be single-minded. Create a community of mental accountability, one that refuses pretense. Pray fervently, out of righteousness. Refuse to dignify or give place to sin. Worship. Seek God's face – not merely His hand. Turn

---

12 J. C. Boyle, quoted by J. I. Packer and Carolyn Nystrom, *Finding Our Way Through Duty to Delight* (Downers Grove, IL: Intervarsity Press, 2006, 2009), 17.

13 Jerry Bridges and Gerald Bridges, *The Chase: Pursuing Holiness in Your Everyday Life* (Colorado Springs, CO; NAV Press, 1993), 11.

from wickedness – and God will honor, forgive and heal.

C. S. Lewis said, "No clever arrangement of rotten eggs ever makes a good omelet." If God is going to serve us up to a watching world as a sweet-smelling savor, then we must be pure. And that means transformational time in the presence of a holy God.

Bonhoeffer lamented, "One is distressed by the failure of reasonable people to perceive either the depths of evil or the depths of the holy."[14] The result is always compromise and spiritual lethargy. Prayer, real prayer, involves personal conferences with a holy God that produce holiness and purity of heart. Sadly, good people, because they are good, are kept from prayer and repentance. They depend on their own moral strength – but these are moralists, not Christians, even if they speak 'christianese.' Bad people, that is, people who lack moral character and resist moral change, resent repentance. They fear the implications of the public admission of failing to line up to Biblical ideals, and, at the same time, they fear the imposition of those standards to their lives.

Tragically, both good and bad people avoid the very thing that makes a good Christian – dependence on God. "The essence of chastity is not the suppression of lust, but the total orientation of one's life towards a goal."[15] God is not looking for perfection! He is looking for integrity and dependence on Him. Grace hems us in to true righteousness – the righteousness of Christ.

---

14   Bonhoeffer, from *Ethics*, Quoted by Charles Ringma, *Seize the Day with Dietrich Bonhoeffer* (Colorado Springs, Colorado: Pinion Press; 2000), See entry for January 20.

15   Bonhoeffer, from *Letters and Papers from Prison*, Quoted by Charles Ringma, *Seize the Day with Dietrich Bonhoeffer*; See entry for January 19.

Discussion Questions

1. We are told "Prayer should be a purifying experience." And Spurgeon notes that prayer makes hearts and homes holy. Do you agree or disagree?

2. Have we refashioned a sacrificial faith into a nurturing faith – deforming it?

3. Talk about the differences between transactional and transformational praying.

4. Which is first – prayer or purity? How do they relate to one another?

5. What does it mean for the church to be a confessional community?

4

Prayer As Perspective

The secret of failure is that we see men rather than God. Romanism trembled when Martin Luther saw God. The 'Great Awakening' sprang into being when Jonathan Edwards saw God. The world became the parish of one man when John Wesley saw God. Multitudes were saved when Whitefield saw God. Thousands of orphans were fed when George Mueller saw God. And He is 'the same yesterday, today, and forever.'

Catherine Marshall said, "One can believe in the divinity of Jesus Christ and feel no personal loyalty to Him at all – indeed, pay no attention whatever to His commandments and His will for one's life."[16] That, of course, is possible only in a cool, distant and intellectual sense. It is not Biblical Christianity. True discipleship calls us out of our narrow world and invites us to embrace a global challenge, the Great Commission. God put Adam in a garden, but He had the globe in mind.

William Carey was a shoe cobbler before he was a missionary. As he labored each day, he kept beside him, on his workbench, a map of the world. He prayed and worked – and worked and prayed. As he worked, he prayed over the world. And God called him to reach that world.[17] That is missions' history! Had his prayer experience been narrow and self-interested, he might have remained a shoemaker. Instead he impacted a nation, and became an icon of inspiration for a veritable army of missionaries. What destiny is the lack of prayer keeping you from?

---

16   Catherine Marshall, *Beyond Our Selves* (Harper Collins Publishers; 1994).

17   Frances Laudrum Tyler. *Pray Ye* (Nashville, TN: Broadman, 1944), 17.

The Disciple's Request: Lord, Teach Us To Pray

Of all the things the disciples might have asked for, what they requested was that Jesus teach them to pray. It was not for instructions on more effective teaching or preaching, healing or doing miracles. They did not ask for water-walking lessons. They asked for instruction on prayer. Why? It was obviously clear to them that the power in the earthly ministry of Jesus – in all he did, teaching, preaching, healing, miracles, and wisdom – was from his life of prayer. His communion with the Father brought forth the Father's glory.

At night, when they were ready to turn in, he was still out somewhere in prayer. In the morning when they arose, at times, he had already slipped away to some quiet place for prayer (Mk. 1:35). On some occasions, he spent the entire night in prayer (Luke 6:12). Jesus did not pray to do ministry. His ministry was prayer. He moved from one place of prayer to another with the glory and power of the Father God flowing out of Him. We focus on what happened in between the prayer sessions of Jesus – the teaching, preaching, ministry, miracles. Things that were obvious. But all of that was possible because of the unobvious, his secret life of prayer. He came to the earth to pray. He was not merely an intercessor, he was the ultimate intercessor. And he ever lives today to make intercession (Heb. 7:25).

The Lord's Response: The Model Prayer

"Teach us to pray!" the disciples asked him. His response was incredibly simple. We call the words that follow "The Lord's Prayer." It might be more properly called "the disciple's prayer" for it is the model he gave us for prayer

(Lk. 11:2-4; Mt. 9:9-13). His prayer is actually found in John 17. So let's look at our prayer model:

After this manner therefore pray ye: Our Father which art in heaven, Hallowed be thy name. Thy kingdom come. Thy will be done in earth, as it is in heaven. Give us this day our daily bread. And forgive us our debts, as we forgive our debtors. And lead us not into temptation, but deliver us from evil: For thine is the kingdom, and the power, and the glory, for ever. Amen (Matthew 6:9-13).

Notice, this prayer begins with God. *"Our Father... your name is holy...let your kingdom come and your will be done."* The prayer ends, *"For thine (Father) is the kingdom, power and glory, for ever!"* So the prayer begins and ends with a focus upon God and his Kingdom. It begins with a reminder that we are to hallow, to revere His name, and it ends with a glory due Him. It begins with a focus upon his will and not the imposition of mine upon Him by prayer. How does your prayer begin and end? Here is the *name* of God, the *rule* of God, the *will* of God that qualifies every petition. In the end, prayer is concerned with the *kingdom* that be-

> *Prayer meetings are dead affairs when they are merely asking sessions; there is adventure, hope and life when they are believing sessions, and the faith is corporately, practically and deliberately affirmed.*
>
> *Norman Grubb*

longs to Him, the *power* that flows and the *glory* due Him.

The End Result: An Altered Perspective

Prayer is a means by which God expands and stretches my perspective. He wants me to see the world as He sees it. So in prayer, we are pulled from the dusty earth to the celestial heaven. We are graciously forced to seek His will and not our own. We catch glimpses through the telescope of time and see eternal implications in what we do, so that our decisions are not rooted in some narrow slice of time that will affect us negatively for all eternity. We are moved out of our narrow little world, and into a larger arena. We are mentored to think relationally, not selfishly and independently.

Watch the movement:

<u>**From**</u>	<u>**To**</u>
Cosmic orphans	Members of the Father's family
Earth	Heaven
Our frailty	His hallowedness and wholeness
My domain	His kingdom
My best wisdom	His will
My directing Him	My surrender to Him
Me	We
Us	Our
Being forgiven	Becoming forgiving
Avoiding temptation	Being liberated from evil
Now	Eternity

Prayer should change our perspective. God wants to inflame our praying. Christ gave us *all authority*. Our mission involves *all nations* – the whole world. As we go, we are to observe *all commands* – that means that our mission involves a well-planned strategy. The uncompleted mission given to the church by Christ is for *all time – "Lo, I am with you always, even to the end of the age"* (Mt. 28:20). God is waiting for some generation, at some point in time, to take seriously all the authority, all His commands, and in faith, to strategically fulfill the mission to reach all nations.[18]

The New Focus: Prayer Re-centers Us

So much of our prayer begins and ends with us. Ultimately, prayer is not about us. It is about God. Of course our stuff is included, because God cares about us. We may ask about daily bread. We may request forgiveness of our debts. We may even ask God to exempt us from temptation and tests, to guard our day so that we do not encounter evil and the Evil One. And yet, we are never instructed to make even these types of requests in the singular, just for us alone.

As we pray using this model, we cannot pray – *"me," "my" or "I."* We must pray – *"our," "us" or "we."* Even more so, the prayer that Jesus taught us begins and ends, not with us, but again with God. Prayer must alter our focus. It isn't the attempt to get God to focus on us. He sees and hears all. The need is for for us to see Him – as Father, as holy, as King, as head of a universal and unstoppable, incomparable Kingdom, as the One who fills the heavens, the earth being too small for Him. As the One who supplies needs, because of his unlimited creative capacity; forgives out of His limitless mercy; guides because of His omniscient oversight of all; and delivers due to his omnipotent and unequaled

18   Ben Jennings. *The Arena of Prayer* (Orland, Florida: New Life Publications, 1999), 26.

power. Prayer must shift our focus from our narrow slice of pain, to see Him. Such a shift in focus takes the spotlight off our problems and causes us to see the solution. Only with a God-focus and perspective are our problems manageable.

The Enlarged Community: Relational Awareness

The prayer that we are given as a model is devoid of narrow personal language, and loaded with corporate and relational language – *"our," "us," and "we."* In asking for daily bread, I must request it for us. In seeking forgiveness, I must do so with a concern for broader, healthy relationships. Only as I am willing to forgive, do I experience the full power of God's forgiveness. God will not allow a mere *transaction* with Him, He is interested in our *transformation*. We will not allow one to isolate the vertical from the horizontal.

> *A holy life does not live in the closet, but it cannot live without the closet.*
>
> E. M. Bounds

Not only does the focus shift from us and our pain to God, but it also is broadened to include others. Prayer can't be a constricted and limited transaction between me and God. Prayer constantly stretches me to be as inclusive and loving as the God to whom I pray. It alters my language from *me,* to *us.* It enlarges my focus from *self,* to *community.* It reminds me that the Father has endowed me with brothers – I am part of a family.

Prayer is about relationships:

- The relationship with God *as Father* – "Our Father."
- The relationship with God *as King* of the Kingdom – "for thine is the kingdom."
- The relationship with God as *the architect of divine purpose* – "thy will be done."
- The relationship with God *as provider* – "give us our daily bread." The phrase "our daily bread" may also be an allusion to the request for "daily provision" typical for the Roman military officer at the beginning of each day. His request and the subsequent supply obligated him to go in the strength of that bread in service to the Emperor.
- The relationship with God *as Judge* who releases us legally from our moral debt and its consequences – "forgive us our debts."
- The relationship with God *as guide and protector* – "lead us not into temptation!" He leads us. He is active in helping us navigate bends and blind-spots in the road.
- The relationship with God *as warrior* – "deliver us!" He delivers us. His hand has gotten us liberty and victory.
- The relationship with *the God of power and glory!*

If prayer became the daily reminder of these simple relationship principles, our lives would be changed. "Most men pray for power, the strength *to do* things. Few people pray for love, the quality *to be* someone," observes Robert D. Foster.

At the heart of the prayer is the relational core –

- Care for the *physical* needs of others: bread;
- Care for the *psychological* health of one another: forgiveness;
- And care for the *spiritual purity and liberty* from the corrupting grip of the Tempter: the spiritual dimension.

It's all here. We are to *give* to others. Here is the physical, felt-need dimension. We are to feed the hungry – and this is something that can't simply be institutionalized. Furthermore, since giving "daily bread" to others is something we are to pray about, it cannot be an act of cool detached care. The greater gift to those who are hungry is not edible manna, but spiritual bread. We must pray for them. Prayer and care are welded together here. Care is a way of acting out our prayer for another. So James would forbid us from praying and blessing the needy by saying, *"Go, I wish you well; keep warm and well fed,"* while we do nothing about the physical need. James asked, *"What good is that?"* (James 2:16). Prayer moves us to act. And yet, action without prayer is simply that – human action, without spiritual conviction. The kind of prayer, Jesus urges, makes every believer a missionary.

Forgiveness is the psycho-social, the priestly and pastoral dimension of prayer. Someone has said, "Resentment is like a glass of poison that a man drinks; then he sits down and waits for his enemy to die." Jesus said,

> *Agree with your adversary quickly, while you are on the way with him, lest your adversary deliver you to the judge, the judge hand you over to the officer, and you be thrown into prison. Assuredly, I say to you, you will by no means get out of there till you have paid the last* penny. (Mt. 5:25-26).

This is a practical piece of advice. Don't carry grudges. Don't allow differences to last. Their effect not only lingers, it festers. Buried here are profound spiritual truths as well. Before you leave another person, after there has been some type of rift in the relationship, create conciliatory ground. Come to agreement – *"Agree with your adversary"* in part or whole. In doing so, you neutralize the conflict, which only multiplies, sometimes both irrationally and exponentially, with the separation of the two parties. Unity pacifies. It appeases. It placates. It mollifies. It soothes. It aborts war and acrimony.

There are four phases to the crumbling relationship here:

- *Conflict* – First, a friend has become an adversary. Something has happened to damage the relationship. The division intensifies and is considered unresolvable by the two parties alone. Their separation from one another, without a sense of reconciliation, exacerbates the issue.

- *Judicial Action* – Now, to settle the conflict, a third party is needed, thus judicial action. The problem is going to be adjudicated in court. The conflict is now open, no longer private, but a matter of public record.

- *Conviction* – Third, an arrest is made. Guilt is determined.

- *Bondage* – Fourth, one of the parties loses his freedom. Placed in prison, he is no longer at liberty. He is in lock-down.

Hidden in the text is a spiritual description of what happens to an infected relationship when there is no forgiveness. Here is the scenario.

- *Conflict* – Two people disagree. The quarrel becomes adversarial. The distance between them intensifies and they fail to come to any kind of agreement. They part company with the division firmly in place.

- *Judicial Action* – The matter ends up in God's court! Heaven pays attention to division – God hates discord. One brother may press the matter before God in prayer, eager to resolve the matter. But the failure to be open to reconciliation and forgiveness, by one or both, peaks God's attention and invites His action.

- *Conviction* – One party bears the greater guilt before God. The Holy Spirit pursues one, and then the other, with conviction. But there is no tender heart of repentance, no openness to change, no willingness to forgive.

- *Bondage* – Suddenly, the relationship is in lock-down. It is no longer free, no longer full of joy. Neither party feels liberty toward or around the other. One, or perhaps both, are now in bondage. The rift may affect families, a whole church, a city or even nations.

In bondage, there is no freedom – to fellowship or to love, to forgive or receive forgiveness. Under conviction, and simultaneously resistant to it, refusing to bend or break before God or the offended brother, the heart grows hard. Rationalizations deepen. Sensitivity to the Spirit is affected. Instead of being the Comforter, the Spirit (Phil. 2:1-4; 2 Cor. 7:6; Isa. 61:1) is forced to correct a resistant saint (John 16:8). In truth, it is worse than that.

One or both parties have placed themselves in harm's way. While God loves, He will not exempt even his children from the consequences of their actions. Grace does not suspend sin's toxic effects. We must not act in ways that God has determined to judge! Built into all sin is some type of consequence from the principle of judgment. Sin has wages (Rom. 6:23). I can minimize sin's impact and more quickly destroy its fruit if I "agree quickly" and avert an adversarial relationship. Nothing furthers psychological health more

> *The one thing above all others that bolts and bars the way into the 'presence chamber' of prayer is unwillingness to forgive from the heart.*
>
> Samuel Chadwick

than forgiving and being forgiven.

What keeps us from pursuing peace, from bearing the olive branch? From first asking for forgiveness? It is usually pride! "Excessive pride, the seat of so much misery and unhappiness, like resentment, results from an inflated ego crying for recognition. Criticism hurts us because we allow too much self to come to the fore."[19] And that causes us to become stiff and unbending, unforgiving and revenge seeking. "Prayer," on the other hand, "helps us step outside ourselves. It is not the precious self that needs to be eradicated, but the egotistical self. After all, "a person wrapped up in himself is a pretty small package."[20]

Hannah More said, "A Christian will find it cheaper to pardon than to resent. Forgiveness saves the expense of anger, the cost of hatred, and the waste of spirit."[21]

Forgiveness is not the dismissal of the wrong. It is the sanity that says that the past, no matter how hurtful and disillusioning, can't be changed. And it is giving up my right to hurt another for hurting me. It is refusing to continue the war. It is the call for a truce, on the spot, then and there.

> Not to forgive is to be imprisoned by the past, by old grievances that do not permit life to proceed with new business. Not to forgive is to yield oneself to another's control...to be locked into a sequence of act and response, of outrage and revenge, tit for tat, escalating always. The present is endlessly overwhelmed and devoured by the past. Forgiveness frees the forgiver. It extracts the forgiver from someone else's nightmare.[22]

---

19 Kermit Olsen. *First Steps in Prayer* (New York: Fleming H. Revell; 1947), 56-57. See also; Sir James Jeans. *The Mysterious Universe* (MacMillan), 57.
20 Quote by John Ruskin. www.goodreads.com.
21 Quote by Hannah More. www.christianquotes.info.
22 Quote by Lance Morrow. www.goodreads.com.

It has been observed that:

Resentment is a form of hurt ego. It is an outgrowth of self-pity. A rebellion against events or people who have thrust at one's pride, interests, ambitions. One who is given to resentment feels that he has been frustrated by an act or event. The way to overcome resentment is to step outside of self.[23]

Charles Allen, the great integrator of psychiatry and theology, says there are four problems that are foremost in humanity – fear, guilt, self-centeredness and the inability to forgive. He says the last one – the inability to forgive – is the hardest to deal with.[24]

To forgive is to commit the matter to God. If the other person is wrong, then the Holy Spirit will convict them. They will end up in God's court, under discipline. They will end up in lock-down, in an emotional prison. God does pursue the guilty. But, he wants us to be agents of release. As we have been forgiven, so should we forgive. Freely we have received, freely we should give.

Finally, the plea of the prayer is for spiritual protection from the Evil One. This is the spiritual dimension. We are not only to pray for our deliverance, but for the hand of God to be on others as they navigate the maze of daily life. "Let them not come into the hand of the Evil One!" Deliver them. This is a prayer for spiritual insight, for wisdom in decisions, for spiritual guidance.

Pray the prayer. Personalize it:

God, you are Father, our Father, my Father, my King and the architect of my life, indeed, all of our lives. You have a

---

23 Olsen, 27.
24 Charles L. Allen. *All Things are Possible through Prayer* (Grand Rapids, Michigan; 1958, 2003), 101.

plan for me – for my family and friends – and I ask today that you direct our steps according to your will. Let me live in a way that glorifies your name, the family name and advances your kingdom. You are my provider, for all my needs today. And in meeting my needs, you want me to be sensitive to the needs of others and me – the hungry and the hurting, the homeless and the have nots. You are my ultimate Judge. I don't want to end up in your courtroom – please, forgive me and may I be a forgiving person. Make me an agent of reconciliation. You are a warrior God, the protector of my life. Keep me from sin. Deliver me from the Evil One. Let me live a life of triumph. And by my example, may I influence others away from sin and out of the grip of evil. Let my life glorify you. Reveal through me your power and your glory. Amen.

In *The Man of La Mancha* the lead character sings the wonderful song, "To Dream the Impossible Dream." He meets Aldonza. Though she is a prostitute, he calls her, "My lady!" And then he declares, "I give you a new name –Dulcinea." He sees her not as she is, but as she can be. It is too much for her. She screams, "Don't call me a Lady. I was born in a ditch by a mother who left me there, naked and cold and too hungry to cry. I never blamed her. I'm sure she left hoping that I'd have the good sense to die. Look at me. I'm no lady. I'm only a kitchen slut, reeking with sweat. A strumpet men use and forget. Don't call me Dulcinea. I am only Aldonza and I am nothing at all!"

Overwhelmed with shame and polluted by guilt, without hope or dignity, Aldonza disappears into the darkness. But the Man of La Mancha is relentless as she withdraws, he objects, "But you are my lady, Dulcinea." Here is the gospel. It is Christ who has come to the earth, searching and calling for His bride, the Church. It is Hosea, calling out to his wife Gomer, who has become a prostitute. It is God calling, "But you are my child." You're a child of God. He loves you, even if you are a lost soul. Find and follow the faith God has for you. You'll be born again and turned into a beautiful blessing to be a blessing soul.

In the last act of the play, the knight is dying. He has been condemned as an outcast. He is considered crazy, insane. His impossible dream is in peril. His heart is broken. And to his dying bed comes a lady. She's beautiful. She is dressed in mantilla and lace. A heavenly choir sings in the background. She prays. He opens his eyes. "Who are you?" he asks. She rises. She stands erect. She answers, "My name? My name is Dulcinea." Aldonza has been born again. She has been transformed. The unbeliever has become a believer. The sinner has become a saint. The impossible has happened. How could such a change take place? It is simple, and yet, profound. She came to believe what the knight believed about her. What the Man of La Mancha believed she could and would become. "I am not what *I* think I am. I am not what *you* think I am. I am what *God* thinks I am." It is only when we get into our head, what Christ says about us, that transformation takes place.[25] I am what God thinks about me! More precisely, I am what I think God thinks about me – what I believe as I pull down the strongholds of the mind and replace them with a godly self-image.

> To dream...the impossible dream...
> To fight...the unbeatable foe...
> To bear...with unbearable sorrow...
> To run...where the brave dare not go...
> To right...the unrightable wrong...
> To love...pure and chaste from afar...

---

25 Robert Schuller. Prayer: *My Soul's Adventure with God* (New York: Image Books; 1995), 216.

To try...when your arms are too weary...
To reach...the unreachable star...

This is my quest, to follow that star...
No matter how hopeless, no matter how far...
To fight for the right, without question or pause...
To be willing to march into hell, for a heavenly cause...

And I know if I'll only be true, to this glorious quest,
That my heart will lie will lie peaceful and calm,
when I'm laid to my rest...
And the world will be better for this:
That one man, scorned and covered with scars,
Still strove, with his last ounce of courage,
To reach...the unreachable star...[26]

Prayer, time with God, alters our perspective!

Discussion Questions

1. With Carey's illustration in mind – ask, "What do we pray for? Does anyone keep a globe near them when they pray?"

2. Note the three qualities to all prayers in the preamble to the prayer Jesus taught - the *name,* the *kingdom* and the *will.* Discuss them.

3. Look at the two columns on prayer on page 50, the movement implied in the 'Lord's Prayer.' Which column do you pray from?

4. Review the relationships with God implied in the prayer Jesus taught on page 57.

5. In Mt. 5:25-26, Jesus addresses relationships and reconciliation. Discuss the moments in the passage from a spiritual perspective.

---

26 Lyrics by Joe Darion, from the song: *The Impossible Dream,* and the Musical, *The Man of La Mancha!* www.stlyrics.com/lyrics/bestofbroadway-americanmusical/theimpossibledream.htm.

5

Prayer as Persistence

Prayer must be aflame.
Its ardor must consume.
Prayer without fervor is as a sun without
light or heat, or as a flower without beauty or
fragrance. A soul devoted to God is a fervent
soul, and prayer is the creature of that flame.
He only can truly pray who is all aglow for
holiness, for God, and for heaven.

E. M. Bounds

Malcolm Muggeridge concluded that the most stunning political fact of the last century was the inability of the USSR, with every means of suppression at its disposal, to destroy the Church within its borders. With only state approved and registered churches open, churches that agreed to comply with state standards, many Christians joined an underground movement.

Years before, the Jews of the exile whose faith had been defined by the temple, with its priesthood and ceremonies, learned to adapt. They contextualized faith in a prayer daily prayer commitment. So these Christians also learned that faith was not a matter of place, a building, but a relationship with the person, Jesus Christ.

Suddenly, personal prayer became a defining feature of their lives. Without public and open faith gatherings, private moments with God came to be cherished. Without abundant Bibles, scrapes of Scripture verses were passed between Christians and hidden in their hearts. When the revolution came, missionaries fled. Churches were closed. Christians were openly persecuted. The treatment of any other group with such disdain would have led to an international human rights crisis. Despite all the persecution and oppression, the church survived. Now the church is more resilient than ever before. It is indestructible. It is the extension of Christ himself.[27]

When George Bush was Vice President of the United States, he attended the funeral of former Soviet boss Leonid Brezhnev. At the end of the ceremony, the widow of Brezhnev stood motionless by the casket of her husband, as if she were in another world. No one could have guessed the moment of conscience she was having. Then, just before the coffin lid was closed, the widow of Brezhnev did a bold and daring thing for that era in the most dominant Communist nation on the face of the earth. As the attending soldier reached to touch and close the coffin lid, the widow of the powerful Communist leader reached inside the coffin, and drew the sign of the cross over her husband's chest.

In the global stronghold of cold atheistic power, this woman, who had stood at the side of one of the most powerful and godless leaders of his time in human history, expressed hope in the cross of Christ. It was an act of civil disobedience. It was an act of bold faith. It was a declaration of dissonance. With the world watching, she boldly stood with and simultaneously against her husband. It was an act of love, and of hope. It was an act of courageous differentiation.

One wonders about the private conversations that might have taken place between them which preceded such a moment. There, in front of the whole world, in the face of global dignitaries, in the shadow of the Kremlin, with Party bosses standing nearby, was proof of enduring faith. It had sur-

---

27 Huston Smith. *Why Religous Matters* (San Francisco: Harper, 2001), 155.

vived under a roof shared with the Soviet Boss, himself. It was evident as a grieving widow reached out to a loving God with the world watching. George Bush said he was deeply moved by her silent protest.[28]

It does not take Communism to create similar suppression. I write this note watching various Thanksgiving festivities on American television – in free America. The root of the holiday is about gratitude to God – the God of the Bible. But no one, not one commentator, not one guest, will dare mention the One to whom we should be grateful.

There is much talk about "what" we are thankful for – family and friends. But no one mentions the "Who" to whom we should be thankful. The repression is so strong, the social conformity so deeply enforced, not by political might, but by mere psychological force, and by collective intimidation, that no one dares cross the line, not even in subtle ways.

Here, the political influencers, with the help of the courts and various private and public educational institutions, have accomplished virtually the same end as did atheistic Communism. In truth, ours is the more terrible form of atheism. It is not the militant and passionate struggle against the idea of God himself, but the practical atheism of everyday living, indifference and languor, inactivity and indolence. Sadly, we encounter these forms of atheism among those who are formally Christian. God has been banished from the public square, and few protest. We lack persistence! We are conformist – to the culture.

There has always been a core of believers in the USSR that refused to conform. They defied the edicts. They worshipped and served the only true and living God. They

---

28 Thomas, 149.

risked their lives to keep the underground church alive. In 1988, Moscow marked the seventieth anniversary of the Bolshevik revolution. As the date neared, Christians in the underground Church began to plead for global intercessors to join them in prayer. For seven years, a number of prayer chains continued relentlessly praying for relief. A number of worldwide Christian agencies set January of that year as a month of prayer. The late Vonette Bright, at the time, chair of the National Day of Prayer Committee, called America to prayer. No one knew what, if anything, would happen. But faith believed that the seventieth year had significance.

The story of every great Christian achievement is in the history of answered prayer.
E. M. Bounds

In the underground church, the mantra had become. "Seventy years is long enough!" Persistent prayer intensified. No one anticipated the shocking results. On the first working day, after that month of prayer by Christians around the world, Premier Mikhail Gorbachev did something that was stunning. He released all religious prisoners across the USSR. It was unthinkable. In one stroke, seventy years of persecution and oppression ended. It was breathtaking. Atheistic Communism had begun its melt-down.

Campus Crusade for Christ immediately translated the JESUS FILM into the Russian language. When the film premiered in Moscow, the Secretary of Education requested copies for Russian public schools. The Academy of Sciences and government departments did the same for their personnel. Mission agencies united under the banner of Co-Mission and for the next five years, they trained 38,000 public school teachers in the former Soviet Republics to teach ethics and morality in what had previously been Communist classrooms. Some 60 percent of the public school teachers throughout the nation trusted Christ as Savior.[29] Persistent prayer paid off. Persistent prayer may have toppled a government.

Similar things have happened here within our boundaries. Two hundred years ago, Supreme Court Justice John Marshall suggested that "the church is too far gone to ever to be redeemed." The few Christians on college campuses convened in secret to avoid persecution. The epidemic of alcoholism – 300,000 drunks in a population of 5,000,000 – plagued America. With the moral slump at its worst in 1794, churches of nearly all denominations rallied to a call for united agreement in prayer. Revival in the churches and moral recovery in the young nation followed. Could that happen again? Not without persistence in prayer!

When Jesus taught on prayer he emphasized persistence. In Luke 18 we read: *"And he spake a parable unto them to this end, that men ought always to pray, and not to faint"* (Luke 18:1).

The purpose of this parable was to encourage prayer – always. Prayer is a constant. It is an ongoing facet of our life in God. There is no spiritual life without prayer, only the simulation of it, only a fake spiritual life, an illusion. Jesus urged men to pray and not to faint or not to give up. It is like breathing. E. M. Bounds urged, "Four things let us keep in mind: God hears prayer, God heeds prayer, God answers prayer. And God delivers by prayer."

---

29 Jennings, 148.

Such prayer demands discipline. A disciple is one under discipline. And discipline is no problem for a free disciple. It *is* a problem for cultural Christians, whose faith is largely superficial "Jesus-talk." Read and study the lives of every great Christian in history, look at the details of their daily schedules, and you will discover a common thread. No saint has ever adorned the church with the beauty of their sanctified life, without displaying the great characteristic of discipline and order. Invariably, discipline, true discipleship, is the universal characteristic of all the outstanding men and women of God. Someone has said, "Men do not decide their future. They decide their habits and their habits decide their future." There are three disciplines in Matthew 6 and they anchor the follower of Jesus Christ.

The three are – giving, prayer and fasting. *Giving* is my relationship to all things external. If you cannot give it away, you do not own it. It owns you. And giving is related to prayer. A grasping heart evidences selfishness in prayer, a clear obstacle to divine answers.

Prayer is my relationship to time and all things eternal. If I do not value time with God here and now, it is a signal of where the heart is. It is either here in the now, or there in eternity; here consumed with the earth, or there in heaven. The one thing that keeps working after we die is the effect of our prayer life. If a Christian does not have time to pray, time to spend alone with God, his life is out of control. He has no discipline over his schedule. He is a slave – to the world's system. God wants an appointment with him, daily. But, he has no time for God. God may choose to ride with him on an errand, or talk with him as he takes his daily shower or does some chore. But God is expected to run along beside him and talk as he, the important human, busies himself with his more essential daily duties. This is life upside down. He is rushing headlong into eternity, evidencing no time to regularly meet God, laying all else aside.

Finally, *fasting* controls all things internal. Hunger is the greatest drive of the body. Subduing the flesh is paramount for spirit-controlled living. Fasting is the sign that spiritual hunger has triumphed over fleshly hunger.

> *Of your faith does not make you pray, have nothing to do with it: get rid of it, and God help thee to begin again.*
>
> C. H. Spurgeon

Here are the keys to control – over time and eternity, prayer; over the flesh and all internal drives, fasting; over all things external, giving. For each of these disciplines there is a promised reward. Persistence in prayer is impossible without discipline. Such ideas are commonly viewed today as legalism.

> It is wrong to say that we are being 'legalistic' when we are concerned with the ordering of our Christian life and with our faithfulness in requirements of scripture reading and prayer. Disorder undermines and destroys the faith.[30]

The Message of Luke 18: Don't Give Up On Prayer

It is interesting that the concern of Jesus was that we might give up on prayer. In fact, prayer is the first thing we

---

30 Bonhoeffer, from *Meditating on the Word*, Quoted by Charles Ringma, See entry for January 31.

tend to give up on. We give up on prayer before we give up on church attendance or preaching, teaching, or other activities. To emphasize persistence in prayer, Jesus tells this interesting story.

> *There was in a city a judge, which feared not God, neither regarded man: And there was a widow in that city; and she came unto him, saying, Avenge me of mine adversary. And he would not for a while: but afterward he said within himself, Though I fear not God, nor regard man; Yet because this widow troubleth me, I will avenge her, lest by her continual coming she weary me* (Luke 18:2-5).

This is one of those stories that move us to "protect" God. It makes Him appear harsh and insensitive. We must storm heaven and bang the door down in order to move Him to answer and even then it seems that he could care less about us. Spurgeon said, "Pray until you can pray. For it is when you think you cannot pray that is when you are praying."

The Meaning of the Parable: Contrast – Not Comparison

As we noted earlier, this parable is not about comparison; it is about contrast. Notice the differences.

The Judge is...	God is...
Insensitive	Sensitive
Cold and hard	Warm and caring
Inconsiderate	Considerate
Unjust	Very Just – even merciful and gracious
Appears biased	Fair
Without respect of men	Loving toward men

| Willing to allow the widow hurt | Not willing that any perish |

This man should not have been a judge. And this woman could not have handpicked a worse scenario than to end up in the jurisdiction of this particular judge. Here again is contrast. In that culture, to be a woman meant that you were disadvantaged socially. But to be a widow was a double disadvantage. A widow who had been married was not as desirable as an unmarried virgin. Without a husband, there may have been no man to be her social protector or advocate. That seems clear from our text. She has an adversary from which she herself cannot get relief. So she turns to the justice system and asks for relief, but she gets no justice. It is not mercy she seeks, only justice. But there is no social system to protect women in this courtroom. Her response is vigilant persistence. She will not give up. She will not be intimidated. She will not be told "No!"

It is here that another contrast is clear between this woman and us:

The woman is...	**And we...**
Determined	Are undetermined
Tireless in persistence	Tire easily of persistent prayer
Refuses to give up	Faint
Continual and consistent	Are sporadic and inconsistent

E. M. Bounds called a prayerless ministry "the undertaker" for God's church. He claimed that "a prayerless Christian will never learn God's truth" – is spiritually discerned. The

Bible is understood when it is read by a man on his knees. And, Bounds said, "a prayerless ministry will never be able to teach God's truth." The truths of God need supernatural energy which comes only by prayer to penetrate darkened hearts.

> Ages of millennial glory have been lost by prayerless church. The coming of our Lord has been postponed indefinitely by prayerless church. Hell has enlarged herself and filled her dire caves in the presence of the dead service of the prayerless church.[31]

The Bottom Line: God Answers People who are Persistent in Prayer

Listen to Jesus again:

And the Lord said, Hear what the unjust judge saith. Shall not God avenge his own elect, which cry day and night unto him, though he bear long with them? I tell you that he will avenge them speedily. Nevertheless when the Son of man cometh, shall he find faith on the earth? (Luke 18:6-8).

The point of the parable is that if a socially disadvantaged widow can move a hard-hearted, insensitive judge by her persistent request, how much more will the prayers of God's people touch Him?

We don't have a hard-hearted judge in heaven. We have a loving Father who longs to hear and answer prayer. Why then are not more prayers answered? The point of the parable is – a lack of persistence. We give up in prayer too easily. God has chosen to use prayer as a character builder! He demands that we "ask and keep-on asking; seek and keep-on seeking; knock and keep-on knocking." Prayer strengthens

---

31   E. M. Bounds, *The Best of E. M. Bounds on Prayer* (Grand Rapids, Michigan: Baker Book House; 1981), 102.

persistence and determination.

Bill Hybels says that God always answers prayer, and that sometimes he says, "No!" When our requests are wrong, unwise for us, or out of Scriptural bounds, God loves us enough to say, "No!" At other times, God says, "Grow!" The problem may not be in the request itself. It is rather that God sees something in us as more important than the immediate answer to our prayer. So He subordinates our prayer request to our growth in grace. "Grow! He bids us." Then there are times when God says, "Slow!" The request is right. And we are right before Him, but the timing is wrong. So God calls us to patience. Then there are those wonderful times when the request is right, we are right, the timing is right – and in such moments Hybels quotes God as saying, "Go!"

God always answers prayer – "No; Grow; Slow or Go!"

In the end, Jesus asked, *"When the Son of Man comes will he find faith on the earth?"* He has not changed subjects. He is reminding us that if persistent prayer has endured, then faith will be alive on the earth. Here is his point – the survival of faith in the earth rises or falls on our persistence in prayer. Without prayer, vibrant faith ceases. Another form of faith may survive, but it will be a twisted and distorted version of New Testament faith. True faith demands prayer. "God's most exquisite gift to man – the crown jewel of His gifts, is the ability to converse with him in prayer."[32]

Thorlief Holmglad was a pastor in Oslo a century ago. Those were dismal years for Norway. As the pastor stepped from his pulpit, his excited custodian saw the look of despair on his face, "There's going to be a revival in this church!" he

---

32   Merv Rosell, quoted by Jennings, 151.

said to the pastor. The pastor turned and faced the empty pews, "Revival? Does this look like revival?" Come with me, the custodian said, leading the pastor to a spot behind the pulpit. "Do you see those water marks on the carpet? Those are tear stains. I have been praying and weeping here for five years. The lord has assured me he is going to send a revival!"

> *I will not let thee go, except thou bless me.*
> *Jacob*

The custodian was not alone. In a nearby city, two sisters were crying out to God for revival. Their burden for renewal had become heavy. "If it is your will for us to continue to pray, then send other intercessors." The two became four. The four became eight. The eight became sixteen. These small pockets of believers persisted in prayer for revival, against all odds. And yet the revival did not begin in the home of the intercessors, nor yet behind the pulpit where the custodian had prayed. It happened in a most unlikely place.

In a Sunday evening youth meeting, filled with restless, disinterested youngsters, a cloud of God's glory appeared visibly to the youth leader. As he struggled to gain the attention of the young people, the white cloud slowly descended from the ceiling. To his dismay and disbelief, the more the presence of the cloud filled the room, the more restless the young people became. Finally, it touched the tops of their heads. Instantly, young people fell to their knees praying, weeping, confessing their sins. The tenor of that youth meeting impacted the adult evening worship service. Adults were themselves weeping and repenting of sin in prayer. Special services were conducted the next evening on Monday. Then on Tuesday. They continued throughout the week. A spirit of brokenness persisted and the revival continued for twelve years. It spread to other churches. Then to other cities and finally to the nation. Some 20,000 people were converted and added to Christ in the city of Oslo alone.[33] Persistence.

Roger Simms was just returning home from military duty and was hitchhiking. To his surprise a shiny new black car stopped to pick him up. He carefully loaded his heavy duffle bag into the back seat and climbed into the front passenger seat where he was greeted by the friendly smile of the driver, a sharp-looking older gentleman.

> "Hello, son. Are you on leave or are you going home for good?"
> "I just got out of the army, and I'm going home for the first time in a long, long time." answered Roger.
> "Well, if you are going to Chicago, you are in luck," smiled the man.
> "I'm not going as far as Chicago, but my home is right on the way to Chicago, so I guess this is my lucky day. Thank you. My name is Roger Simms."
> "Mr. Simms, I'm Mr. Hanover."
> "Nice to meet you sir. Do you live in Chicago?"
> "Yes. I live there and have a business there."

They continued to exchange stories. As they got closer to Roger's home, Roger, who was a Christian, felt impressed that he should broach the subject of faith. "Mr. Hanover, have you ever heard of the difference between religion and Christianity?"

> "I was always under the impression Christianity was a religion," replied Hanover.
> "Not really, said Roger. You see, Religion is always

---

33   Jennings, 171-172.

spelled '*DO*'. Everyone into religion is always trying to do something to please God and be acceptable. The only problem is nobody can know for sure if they've done enough. In fact the bible tells us, we can't do enough to be acceptable. Where religion is spelled '*DO*,' Christianity is spelled '*DONE*'. On the cross, Christ finished everything for us. He did everything for us to be acceptable to God. He even shouted from the cross, 'It is finished!' Which could be translated 'paid in full.' He paid the penalty for our sin. All we need to do is receive the gift he has given us. Mr. Hanover, it isn't enough to know this, the Bible says we have to receive it. '*Yet to all who received him, to those who believed in his name, he gave the right to become children of God*' (John 1:12). Mr. Hanover, would you like to receive Christ as your Savior?"

Even as Roger framed the question he realized, Mr. Hanover was pulling his big car off the shoulder of the road and coming to a stop. *Here it is*, Roger thought, *he's going to ask me to get out*. But he didn't. Mr. Hanover didn't even look at Roger. He bowed his head and quietly began to weep. After a moment, Roger asked again, "Mr. Hanover, would you like to ask Christ into your life?"

Mr. Hanover nodded an affirmation, then said, "What do I say?"

Roger led Mr. Hanover in a simple prayer asking for forgiveness for sins, and asking Christ to be Savior, and thanking him for what he did for him on the cross.

> "Thank you for talking to me about this, Roger. What you said is exactly what I needed to hear. I thought I would never be able to be a Christian. I thought somehow I needed to change everything. Now I understand it isn't up to me, but Christ. This is the best thing that ever happened to me."

After some more talking, Mr. Hanover drove to Roger's

house, gave him his business card, thanked him again and dropped him off.

But that's not the end of the story. Five years went by. Roger got married and had a child. One day, while he was packing for a business trip to Chicago, he found the business card that Mr. Hanover had given him five years before. He decided that while he was in Chicago he would try to look him up.

In Chicago, Roger looked up Hanover Enterprises. The building was impressive. When he asked the receptionist if he could see Mr. Hanover, she replied that would be impossible. He tried to let her know that they were old friends.

"If you are old friends, then you can see Mrs. Hanover," she replied.

A little disappointed, Roger was led to an office down the hall. A woman in her fifties was sitting behind a huge oak desk. She extended her hand, "You knew my husband?"

Roger explained how he had met Mr. Hanover about five years ago, when he was so kind as to give him a ride home after his military service had ended.

A strange look came over Mrs. Hanover's face, and she asked, "Would you be able to tell me what date it was, by any chance, when Mr. Hanover gave you a ride?"

Thinking it a strange question, Roger answered nonetheless, because he knew precisely the day of his discharge, and said so. "It was May 7th, the day of my discharge, Ma'am."

Mrs. Hanover seemed even more peculiar. "Did anything special happen on your ride? I mean did anything unusual take place?" she asked.

Roger hesitated, unsure whether this woman would now

be angry at him over what had taken place. Was she an atheist who was angry at her husband's change? Had this been a source of contention between them? For a moment, he was tempted to withhold the details of the private prayer time. But again, he felt impressed to tell her what happened. "Yes Mrs. Hanover, something very special happened that day. Your husband accepted the Lord Jesus as his Savior. I explained to him the gospel, and he pulled over and wept and asked Jesus to come into his life. He was very happy about it."

Suddenly, Mrs. Hanover began to weep uncontrollably. *What was going on here?* Roger could hardly guess. He simply put his hand on her shoulder and let her regain her composure. She was finally able to explain her behavior.

> I grew up in a Christian home. My husband did not. I was warned not to marry a non-believer, but I loved him. I prayed for him all these years. I was sure God would bring him around. On May 7th I thought God had failed me. He didn't answer my prayers. Mr. Hanover was killed on May 7th in a horrible head-on collision. He never arrived home. I haven't been the same since. I stopped trusting God. How could God allow this to happen? How could God take him away and not answer all those prayers? I've been blaming God for these last 5 years.

Persistent prayer pays off – even when we fail to see the results. Mr. Hanover died a believer. And Mrs. Hanover recovered her faith. Never give up on God or the promises he has made, or the people we have entrusted to him in believing prayer.

Discussion Questions

1. Why do people give up on prayer?

2. What are the three central disciplines noted by Jesus?

3. Discuss Spurgeon's advice "Pray until you can pray. For it is when you think you cannot pray that is when you are praying."

4. Why does God require persistence in prayer?

5. In what ways are we like the woman in the parable of Jesus? In what ways are we not like her?

6
Power Through Prayer

*There is nothing the devil dreads
so much as prayer?*

The Kneeling Christian

*There is a marked absence of travail.
There is much phrasing, but little pleading.
Prayer has become a soliloquy instead of
a passion. The powerlessness of the church
needs no other explanation...*

*To be prayerless is to be
both passionless and powerless.
They who prevail in the secret place of the
Most High cannot be beaten anywhere.*

Samuel Chadwick

T. W. Hunt, the great Baptist leader, said, "Prayerlessness is a statement to God that we do not believe that spiritual forces have the power to affect a world created by a spiritual being."[34] This is what the godless believe – that the real power is in the visible, the seen, the measurable dimension. It is pointless to pray "for Kings and all who are in authority" if we do not believe that our prayers affect thrones.

In the archives of press releases from the days of World War II comes the following:

> Twelve boys, who met every Sunday for three years after the fall of Bataan to pray for divine guidance for the Allied leaders, today had the personal thanks of an American General. The boys – too young to fight – decided 10 days after the fall of Bataan that they would do something to help victory. They decided it would be prayer. Major General Edward P. King, the man who was forced to surrender Bataan and then make the death march, visited the boys yesterday. He was back from more than two years in a Japanese prison camp. He said he wanted to thank the 13-to-14 year-old youngsters personally. He told them that faith means more than anything else to

---

34 T. W. Hunt, *The Doctrine of Prayer* (Nashville, TN: Convention Press; 1986), 91.

soldiers facing death. 'Men who do not expect to live become very close to God,' King said. 'Men who avoid the chaplain most during peacetime will walk ten miles for one when he expects to die." King said he wished the men on Bataan had known about the Atlanta prayer band. He said he was certain that their weekly prayers had been a mighty influence.

The boys prayed – and wrote letters. They prayed for Allied leaders regularly and sent prayer support letters. As they listened to Major General King, their faces glowed. Their bold prayer band had already received letters of thanks from General MacArthur, Admiral Nimitz, Field Marshal Montgomery, Winston Churchill and President Roosevelt. The boys started their weekly prayer effort with one name on their prayer list. Before they finished their three-year prayer vigil, they had 150 names on their list. Every Sunday they would repeat every one of the names with bowed heads and reverent hearts. It had been the words of General MacArthur that had led the boys to form the group. "With divine guidance," MacArthur had said, "we cannot fail." That was when the boys decided that prayer was mightier than the forces of war. Admiral Nimitz wrote in August, 1942, "The prayers of these boys for ultimate victory will be answered." Roosevelt sent a picture weeks before his death with the inscription, "To the boys of the Bataan prayer band. From their friend."[35]

Nothing is clearer in the New Testament than the connection between prayer and spiritual power. Armin Gesswein observed in his book, *Everything by Prayer*, that "Pentecost did not come through a preaching service; Pen-

---

35 Frank Laubach. *Prayer – The Mightiest Force in the World* (New York: Fleming H. Revell; 1946), 9-10.

tecost came to a prayer service. From Pentecost to Patmos, God never departs from the pattern."

E. M. Bounds says, "God's Word is a record of prayer – of praying men and their achievements, of the divine warrant of prayer and of the encouragement given to those who pray." Bounds says, "The success of His work in this world, is committed to prayer...praying men have been God's vice regents on earth...."[36] The book of Acts is a book about a praying church. Notice the connection between prayer and the great break-through moments in the history of the early church.

> *We think of prayer as a preparation for work, or a calm after having done work whereas prayer is the essential work. It is the supreme activity of everything that is noblest in our personality.*
> Oswald Chambers

1. Prayer Invites the Holy Spirit

In Acts 2, a prayer meeting matured on the Day of Pentecost. Into that prayer meeting, the Holy Spirit descended. The whole building appeared to be on fire. The sound of a heavenly storm filled the room, loud enough to be heard across the city. It was the roar of the slain lamb, the Lion of

---

36 Bounds, 11.

the Tribe of Judah. He was back, by the Spirit, to empower his church. Tongues of fire danced on each of the heads of the 120 newborn, Spirit-filled saints. For the first time since Babel, the whole earth was linguistically united. Everyone heard the message in their own tongue. At the end of the day, 3000 souls were reaped and the New Testament Church was launched.

2. Prayer Releases Healing Power

In Acts 3, it was to a prayer meeting that Peter and John were headed. It was near the hour of 3:00 p.m., the time the evening sacrifice was prepared and offered at the temple. Across Jerusalem and the Jewish world, it was an hour of prayer. Entering the temple compound, at the Gate Beautiful, the pair of Spirit-filled apostles encountered a lame man begging alms. Peter was both compassionate and penniless, but he was not poor. *"Silver and gold have I none, but such as I have give I thee. In the name of Jesus rise and walk"* (Acts 3:6).

Immediately, the Bible says, his ankles received strength and the lame man rose and walked. It was one more frustration for the Jewish leaders – their Passover had been affected by a siege of darkness and an earthquake that rent the precious and sacred veil between the holy place and the Most Holy Place into two pieces, and it was at this same hour of prayer, fifty days earlier. All they could do was sew it back together. Their feast of the first-fruits had been overshadowed by the Resurrection rumors that encircled the city, three days later. Their Feast of Pentecost had also been interrupted by a prayer meeting of the 120 and the thousands who came to believe that Jesus was not dead, but alive. Now, there was another disturbance, a lame man healed in the name of Jesus. They couldn't get rid of Jesus. He kept popping up everywhere. Crucify him and he rises from the dead, and then multiplies himself. First, there are 120 of Him. Then 3000. Soon, the number will embrace 5000 households, ten-to-twenty percent of the entire population of the city. The great irony of Acts 3 is the interruption of a prayer meeting in the temple by an answer to prayer. The lame has been healed. But the answer to prayer is resisted and the two men who prayed, Peter and John, are persecuted.

> *Do the angels veil their faces before You, and shall I be content to prattle through a form with no soul and no heart?*
>
> *C. H. Spurgeon*

3. Prayer Shakes Sacred Space and Emboldens the Church

The threats are intensified and the pressure sends the faithful to their knees. They gather for prayer. And into that prayer meeting, recorded in Acts 4, the power of God comes in such force that *"the place where they were assembled was shaken."* The supernatural character of the death and Resurrection of Christ was objectified so many times – the darkness in the ninth hour at the time of his death, the rent veil, the stone rolled away, the linen shroud left like a caterpillar after the butterfly had crawled out of his cocoon, the napkin neatly folded, the multiple appearances of Christ, the ascension, the coming of the Spirit with objective signs: audible wind (a sound), visible fire (sight), empowerment and supernatural speech (languages), fire on each of their heads (the personal attachment of the Spirit), the healing of the lame man (Acts 3). And now, the place, the physical space around them was vibrating. And there was another effect, arguably, a more important one. It was the extraordinary change in the disciples – boldness, articulate abilities previously unknown, persuasive skills. They had changed. They had power and capacities they had not previously possessed.

4. Prayer Renews Church Growth and Unifies

In Acts 6, the effect of the growth of the church was now staggering. The care for the poor and the disadvantaged was a major portion of their work. Despite all their efforts, the Greeks among them felt that they were being slighted. For the first time, ethnic differences allowed the suggestion of prejudice. It was a stunning charge. Were they not one? Had they not been forged together through the blood of Christ into a new man, a transcendent identity?

The apostles recognized suddenly that they had allowed an imbalance to occur in their own lives. They had been drawn into the overwhelming work of *public ministry,* at the expense of the priority of *private time with God.* Their personal growth, and the spiritual and relational health of the Church itself, and that of the people, demanded a deeper root system than they were nurturing in private times with God. The diagnosis seems foreign to us, meaning that the health of the church, that the quality of relationships in the church, is somehow tied to the prayer life of the leaders – what an idea!

They made a wise decision. They would appoint men to carry on supporting ministries. And to those men would be committed the ministry to the disadvantaged. The men were to be wise and filled with the Spirit. They were to be mature and to reflect diversity in ethnic leadership. The apostles recommited themselves to the priority of prayer and the word. They recognized that church affairs and business had wrongly subordinated their apostolic call. They were ordered to prayer and the word, not to tables. When the balance was restored, the church again saw growth and division was healed.

Rabbi Liebman died the young age of 41, only three years after the release of his immensely popular book, *Peace of Mind*. What an irony! After the release of that popular book, Charles Allen wrote, "He was swamped with people seeking peace. His mail was heavy, his telephone rang constantly, people came to him steadily all day and even to his home at night. He was a kind-hearted man..."[37] Evidently, he could not turn them away. In the end, he lost the peace, the *shalom*, that he himself had discovered and written about. So it is, when we completely give ourselves to others, no matter how noble our intent, and we have little or no time left for God, we end up having nothing to give to people.

5. Prayer Delivers

Herod, the grandson of Herod the Great who ruled dur-

---

37 Allen, 43.

ing time Jesus was born, wanted to retain the favor of the Jewish people and their leaders. While he had little hope of having them like him, or even respect him, he knew certain favors would curry peace. And Herod wanted peace in his province.

In Jerusalem, He even observed certain aspects of Judaism, acting publicly as if he were an observant Jew. In his short reign of three years (A.D. 414), his means of countermanding Jewish distaste for foreign rule and for his Roman background, not to mention his Edomite ancestry, was his observance of Jewish customs and public support of the Jewish faith.[38]

It was, however, all an act. Noticing Christians as an unpopular dissident sect within Judaism, a source of social and religious dissension, at least to

> Is the Son of God praying in me, or am I dictating to Him?... Getting things from God ... is a most initial form of prayer; prayer is getting into perfect communion with God. If the Son of God is formed in us by regeneration, He will press forward in front of our common sense and change our attitude to the things about which we pray.
>
> Oswald Chambers

---

38 William Neil, *The Acts of the Apostles*, 148.

Jewish leaders, and believing them to be no more than that, he made a fatal decision. He saw the opportunity to gain Jewish favor, particularly with the leaders, by executing the prominent members of the "heretical Christian sect." That action, he evidently believed, should convince Jewish leaders of his sensitivity to them. Perhaps, they would be more favorably disposed toward him. If not, he would have another bargaining chip on his side of the table.

So in Acts 12, the church came under another siege of imperial persecution. James, the brother of John, and a prominent apostle, was martyred. By beheading James, Herod was making a gesture of solidarity with the Jewish majority. It was a public relations ploy to demonstrate his feigned loyalty to Judaism. The Feast of Unleavened Bread was just beginning when Peter was also arrested (12:3). The seven-day period was inclusive of the Passover (12:4). Peter was to remain in jail until the festival cycle was completed. Then, Herod evidently, planned to place Peter on trial and execute him as he had James. He preferred to wait until the festival was over. As in the time of Jesus, the Jewish leaders constituted a small minority and their opinion did not always represent that of the general population. Another public execution during a sacred season could cause repercussions. Remember, the chief priests had sought to avoid the execution of Jesus during the festival of Unleavened Bread fearing a public riot (Mark 14:2).

So Peter was held in prison during the Feast of Unleavened Bread and the Passover. The whole story represents an irony. Peter, a Jew, was imprisoned on the Passover, the great, cheerful day of liberty from the shackles of slavery. He was confined, not free. The Jewish people, delivered from slavery, were now making prisoners of their own brothers during the season of liberation. Luke seems intent on pointing out the irony.[39] Yet, Peter was not fretting. He was sleeping soundly! Tomorrow, he might die, but tonight, he would sleep like a baby.

Herod had taken every precaution to make sure that Peter did not escape. He had probably been informed that Peter was once before placed in custody only to be found free without an explanation (5:19-24). The location of Peter was probably the Antonia Fortress, a military barracks that later housed Paul for a brief period (21:31-23:32). That fortress complex was conjoined to and overlooked the temple. Peter was such an important prisoner, he was guarded by four squads of four soldiers each, probably on a rotating basis. He had never had so much attention. Luke notes that Peter was sleeping peacefully on the eve of his trial and execution (12:6). He had faith that his life was safe in Christ.

The church gathered for prayer. And God sent an angel to Peter. Acts 12:6 says the apostle *"...was sleeping between two soldiers, bound with two chains, and sentries (plural) stood guard at the entrance of the prison."* Suddenly, the cell was filled with light. The angel manifested to Peter, struck him on the side to awaken him. "Quick, get up!" he said, and the chains fell off Peter's wrists. The angel again struck him on the side and said to him, *"Put on your clothes and sandals...Wrap your cloak around you and follow me"* (Acts 12:8-9). Peter did so, but apparently stunned. Suddenly, the remainder of his chains fell off – here again was the power of God objectified. Peter followed the angel through very real bars and physical objects. For these brief

---

39   William H. Willimon, *Acts*, 112.

moments, Peter's physical body was endowed with powers that transcend the natural. At first, Peter must have thought he was having a dream or vision. The Scripture says, *"They passed the first and second guards and came to the iron gate leading to the city."* Not only was he endowed with power to defy natural obstacles, but he was endowed with invisibility. To some, this is beyond belief. But there is more.

Standing before the gate, a very real physical obstruction, the gate *"opened for them by itself, and they went through it"* (12:9-10). Together, the angel and Peter walked the length of one street, and suddenly the angel left him, he was gone. It was at this moment, that Peter *"came to himself"* (12:11). He would say to himself at that moment, *"Now I know without a doubt that the Lord sent his angel and rescued me from Herod's clutches and from everything the Jewish people were anticipating"* (12:11). The Jewish authorities were anticipating Herod's execution of Peter, but it was not to be. Another power was at work. It was more than mere angelic intervention. It was the hand of God Himself, delivering, for His kingdom progress.

Now free, Peter headed for the home of Mary, the mother of Mark (12:12). The absence of the mention of her husband is a clue that she may have been a widow. Her home was a place where believers gathered, and that night they had come together for a prayer meeting.

All that King Herod could do and had done, in the end, could not bind Peter. His life was not in the hands of the king. He was not subject to the clutches of iron shackles or hardened soldiers. He escaped, in spite of Herod's determined intent to keep him securely in stocks. The contrast is striking – Herod has no power, God is in charge.

The church was praying – and God answered. There is power through prayer. An angel released Peter from prison, but prayer fetched the angel. Only when Peter reached the gate at the home of Mary (an indication that she did not live in a simple home), was he met by the only gate or door that he could not freely pass through – another irony. Rhoda, Mary's household servant, answered the door. The church was still on their knees, praying. Rhoda, also a believer, was joyfully shocked to see Peter. She was so surprised that she left him outside, without opening the gate for him.

Inside, she attempted to convey the message that the prayers of the group had been heard – Peter was not only free, he was at the door. Here we meet another contradiction. The very sincere believers who were earnestly praying that God would intervene and spare Peter could not believe Rhoda's report. "You're out of your mind," they told her. When she kept insisting that it was so, they said, "It must be his angel." Beyond prayer and faith, mixed with angelic intervention and the temporary endowment to Peter of transcendent abilities, is the sovereignty of God. Prayer, in one sense, has no power. God has the power. But it is prayer that seems so often to link supernatural intervention on earth with sovereign action from heaven. God works His purposes in ways that are beyond our understanding.

The whole story is delightfully disarming. It is far from being some formula for miracles that might be repeated. It is not a showcase of neat and ideal faith and prayer. It is gloriously ragged.

1. Peter was confused and stunned by the angelic intervention, even though he had seen it before.

2. Peter was delivered, stood at the door, the answer to the

prayers of the church, but he couldn't get in. His knocking must have grown more and more intense, as he banged on the door.

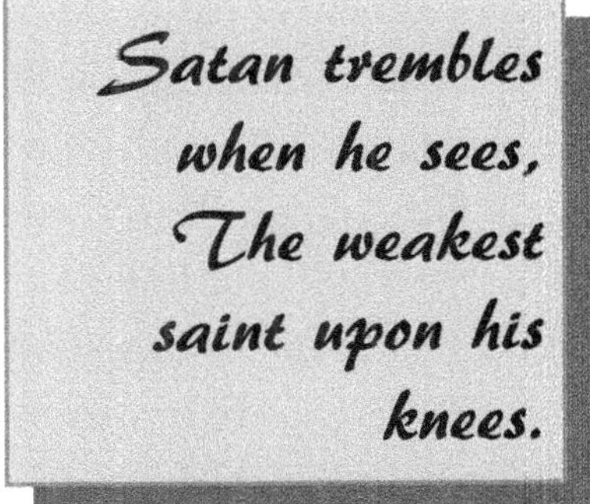

3. Rhoda, the servant, without status, saw Peter and responded in faith. Then she joyfully forgot to open the door for him.

4. The brothers and sisters inside refused to believe the testimony of the servant, Rhoda. Whoever was at the door could not be Peter, he was in prison. This they believed, even though they had fervently prayed for him. The answer was too miraculous, too immediate.

5. Despite the dismissive attitude, Rhoda, a mere servant, holds her ground. She, the least among them, gets to make the announcement. She, the servant, probably only a slave, is the first to believe. "You are out of your mind," they chide her. But she is persistent.

6. With utter astonishment, they finally open the door and let Peter inside.[40]

Peter, after what might have been only a momentary celebration, instructed the group to send word to James, the brother of Jesus, noticeably absent from the prayer meeting, and then Luke records, *"He left for another place"* (12:17). He must have known that Herod would turn the city upside down searching for him. He would not endanger them by remaining with them. Some deliverance is by supernatural intervention. Another part is by common sense. Other apostles may have also left the city for a short season as well. James had the task of steering the church through the tur-

---

40 Longenecker, 410.

bulent season of persecution.

The next morning, there was no small stir about Peter's escape (12:18). The soldiers who were charged with his custody faced death. Herod conducted a thorough search and when he could not find Peter, he tortured the guards to see if they had any information and then had them executed (18:19). The Code of Justinian, from a later period, notes that a guard who allows a prisoner to escape was subject to the same penalty the escaped prisoner would have suffered.

God intervened. Peter experienced liberation in the Passover season – a liberation connected again to angelic activity and power through prayer.

6. Prayer and the King

Herod and the conspiring Jewish leaders had experienced another set-back at the hand of the Sovereign God. And God was not finished showing His dominion. Marcus, the governor of Syria and Herod entered into a dispute that demanded Herod's attention,[41] involving Tyre and Sidon. A peace agreement was reached, and the occasion of the new covenant demanded a celebration at which Herod spoke. Herod arrayed in royal apparel, sat on his throne and rose to address the crowd. Luke records, when Herod finished his speech, the audience heralded him as a Divine. *"This is the voice of a god, not of a man"* (12:22). Herod, a few months prior, had been confronted with the mystery of Peter's release. He must have heard the stories circulating in the streets about the nature of the release. He had seen the fingerprints of God, but he chose to ignore them. Now, he was smitten with a fatal illness for his refusal to acknowledge or

---

41 *Antiquities* 19:339-342.

"give praise to God" (12:23). Herod, Luke says *"was eaten by worms and died"* (12:23) a ghastly death. The miracle was not simply to rescue Peter. It was a message to Herod regarding the reality of God. Sadly, Herod's blindness was deadly.

There is another account of these events by Josephus. He indicates that Herod was smitten with the strange illness at a festival in honor of Caesar at Caesarea, as Luke also indicates in Acts. This festival occurred every five years. Other provincial officials and important dignitaries were in attendance. The date of the festival would have been August 1, A.D. 44, the emperor's birthday, a matter of months after the incident with Peter.[42] On that day, Herod, according to Josephus, donned a silver robe and entered the theater early in the morning, looking resplendent. The flattering mobs, saying he was a god, were not rebuked.[43] Almost immediately after the idolatrous honor, Herod experienced severe cramps. Five days later, he was dead.[44]

Luke and Josephus, the Jewish historian, both attribute Herod's death to Divine judgment. The three stories – James, Peter and Herod – seem to be purposely strung together in the Scripture to make a point. First, God allowed one, James, a significant leader, to die. He thus sent a message to the Church and to us, that not all will be spared. Following Christ demands a cross. There is a risk involved in being

---

42 Peter's release from prison and the death of James would have been in the Passover season – March or April, and Herod's sickness would have taken place in August.

43 Josephus observes: *Upon this the king did neither rebuke them, nor reject their impious flattery* (*Antiquities* 19:346).

44 Herod's death is placed in A.D. 44, in the fourth year of the Roman emperor Claudius.

a disciple. Second, he spared Peter in a stunning miracle that defied reason. He did that in answer to prayers prayed by a church that hardly had the faith to believe in the very prayer they

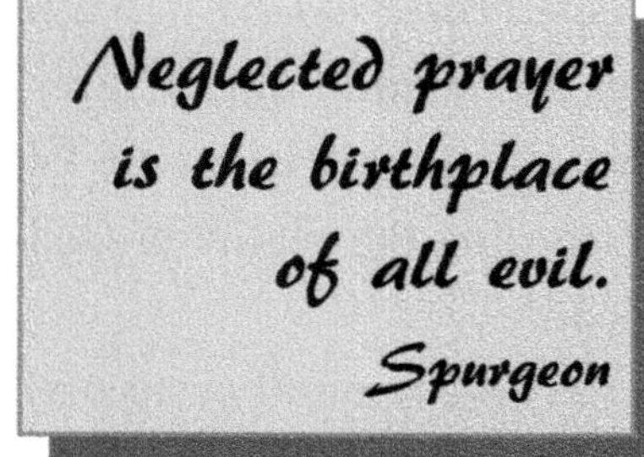

were praying. Under the siege of persecution, fresh from the death of James, and facing the loss of Peter, their faith was feeble. But, God still heard their prayer. Third, he turned to the King, to Herod, and he sent his angel to smite Him. One angel delivers. Another judges. Overall, God is sovereign, over the church and the state. And the administration of his sovereignty in the earth is somehow connected to prayer!

At times, he moves miraculously, to protect the church and judge those who oppose his purposes. God healed the lame man at the temple gate, and then struck Ananias dead. He delivered Peter from Herod's clutches, and then struck down King Herod himself. With the death of Herod, God put a stop to his conspiracy with Jewish leaders against the Church. The nature of Herod's death underscored the superficial and hypocritical nature of his Judaism. He was not a worshipper of Yahweh. He thought of Himself as a god. The whole affair created a chilling effect against the future persecution of the church, and empowered the faith of the little flock.

Luke says, after the death of Herod, "...*the word of God continued to increase and spread*" (12:24).[45]

---

45 www.wcg.org/lit/bible/acts/acts12.htm.

7. Prayer Births Mission

In Acts 13, the Church was gathered in prayer. They were ministering to the Lord. And in that context of worshipful waiting, the Holy Spirit spoke to the Church, *"Separate Barnabas and Saul for the work to which I have called them."* It was a significant word, whether by tongues and interpretation or the prophetic, the effect was the same. The church at Antioch was to give birth. They had been blessed with wonderful leaders. Barnabas, such a conciliatory personality, had been sent from Jerusalem. He had retrieved Saul from Tarsus and employed him in a teaching capacity. Five men are mentioned as prophet-teachers. But it was time for the church that had been enjoying such a rich teaching and leadership team to give them up. They had received, now they must give. Barnabas, who came to them from Jerusalem; and Saul, who came from Tarsus, will be given away to others. The church at Antioch would make it possible for them to "go forth," to "be sent," which is the essence of the apostolic. It is not only the Antioch church that is now called to greater maturity, it is church at large. What will Jerusalem think when it hears that Antioch is sending forth their own apostles? The church as a whole is coming of age.

Into sessions of corporate waiting, of soaking prayer, comes the word of the Lord. It is not born in planning sessions, but in a prayer meeting. The church is to be led not by heads, but by hearts. Not by calculating reason, but by the Spirit. Such things seem worlds away from where we are now. Soren Kierkegaard noted,

...Christ did not appoint professors, but followers. If

> Christianity...is not reduplicated in the life of the person expounding it, then he does not expound Christianity, for Christianity is a message about living and can only be expounded by being realized in men's lives.[46]

It is to be lived, not debated. It is to be experienced, more than it can be explained.

The matter was not simply an inspired utterance and a quick reaction. They tested "the word." They acted on the word only after a season of independent and individual "prayer and fasting." What if every call, every missionary couple, every minister or evangelist, church planter or worker was sent only after individual members of the congregation invested personal prayer combined with fasting? What a precious idea this is. First, there is corporate prayer – and a word from the Lord. Then, there is private prayer – with fasting, a search for discernment, a sincere desire to corroborate the message, to find it authentic, but nevertheless, to test it. Such decisions affect lives. Words should be tested when they redirect human destinies. The whole church has a stake in this decision. Here is prayer – and more prayer. Here is spirit-direction, and the greater confirmation of spirit-direction. Only then, does the church lay hands on the two men and send them forth into apostolic ministry. Don't miss the simple point. Apostolic ministry is birthed and confirmed in prayer. The expanding mission of the Church rides on the back of a praying church. Saul is transformed into an apostle – out of a prayer meeting. And Barnabas is commissioned again, having first been sent from Jerusalem.

---

46 Søren Kierkegaard, Peter Preisler Rohde, *The Diary of Soren* (Citadel Press, 1960), 117.

8. Prayer Rocks the Jailhouse with Liberating Power

In Acts 16, Paul and Silas arrived in Philippi. They enquired about believers in the city and heard about "a place of prayer." They arrived at the site of the prayer meeting, down by the river. There, they witnessed to the women who constituted the prayer meeting. Lydia, a worshipper, but not yet a Christian, opened her heart and home. Following the model of Jesus (Luke 10; Mt. 10), they had found a house of peace and from there they would launch their ministry in the city.

In the midst of their ministry, they had attracted unwanted attention from a demonized slave-girl. She had become a virtual street-crier in their behalf, an endorsement Paul hardly cherished. He finally became so troubled that he turned around and said to the spirit, *"In the name of Jesus Christ I command you to come out of her!"* At that moment the spirit left her. The exorcism diminished the power of the slave girl to tell fortunes, and so her owners seized Paul and Silas and dragged them before the magistrates.

They found no sympathizers among the crowd, Jew or Gentile. The folks of the city joined the public attack. Paul and Silas had a sagging popularity rating. The magistrates found them guilty and ordered them to be stripped and beaten. Afterward, they were thrown not only into prison, but placed in the inner cell under strict guard with their feet fastened in irons. The scene, as we noted earlier, is far too common for first-century preachers.

At midnight, the two apostles had a prayer meeting. Luke says they *"were praying and singing hymns to God and the other prisoners were listening to them."* They must have been a curious site – beaten, bloodied, in pain, untreated, with open wounds and every reason to rail at the authorities and complain. Instead, they sang. They talked to God – to the invisible God. It is no odd thing for us, but in a day of idolatry, talking to an invisible God was a strange thing! *"Suddenly there was such a violent earthquake that the foundations of the prison were shaken."* God was home, and He answered His mail. The force of the quake was so great that *"at once all the prison doors flew open, and everybody's chains came loose."* Notice the idea of liberation again – all doors open, as if by an invisible hand. And everyone's chains come off. That is miraculous. All are freed.

> The prayers of God's saints are the capital stock in heaven by which Christ carries on his great work upon the earth. The great throes and mighty convulsions on earth are the results of these prayers. Earth is changed, revolutionized; angels moved on more powerful, more rapid wing, and God's policy is shaped as the prayers are more numerous, more efficient.[47]

The jailer, who had managed not only to ignore the fresh wounds of his newest incarcerated guests, but also to tune out their songs in the night, suddenly woke up. When he discovered the open prison doors, he assumed the worst. They had all escaped. He knew the penalty for his negligence would be death. He preferred suicide. He drew his own sword and was about to kill himself when Paul shouted, *"Don't harm yourself! We are all here!"* Everyone is free. Everyone will live. Paul restrained the prisoners from fleeing, thereby putting at risk the life of the jailer. He was not saved because

---

47 Bounds, 76.

of the dazzling power of God in the earthquake. He was not saved by his exposure to truth in the preaching of Paul. He was uninterested in the message of Paul and Silas. He chose not to explore the reasons that put them in his jail. What touched him was neither power nor truth. What touched him was love. Their concern for his life. Their willingness to stay in the cell as if they were still chained, so that he would not lose his life – that opened his heart. He took Paul and Silas to his own home, received Christ, was baptized, and became a follower of Jesus Christ.

The power of God through prayer is a river flowing through the book of Acts. In case you missed the points, let's review them again:

- In Acts 16, as they pray, God looses stocks and bonds, and sets prisoners free.
- In Acts 13, a time of prayer facilitates the operation of spiritual gifts and releases the apostolic.
- In Acts 12, prayer is the process by which God chooses to send angels on missions in our behalf, to open the prison doors for Peter. And the resistant king dies there as well.
- In Acts, 6, prayer is the context in which division is healed, the place where we recenter ourselves.
- In Acts 4, God shakes up the place where they assemble in prayer.
- In Acts 3, prayer invites the miraculous healing power of God.
- In Acts 2, prayer opens a city up to a visitation of God!

There is incredible power through prayer!

God shapes the world by prayer. Prayers are deathless. The lips that uttered them may be closed in death, the heart that felt them may be may have ceased to beat, but the prayers live before God, and God's heart is set on them and prayers outlive the lives of those who uttered them; outlive a generation, outlive an age, outlive a world. That man is the most immortal who has done the most and the best praying.[48]

THE CLOUD

A few years ago, Spencer January went to be with the Lord. I have friends who knew him – knew him as a wonderful Christian man. This is his story:

It was a morning in early March, 1945, a clear and sunny day. I was 24 years old and a member of the U.S. Army's 35th Infantry Division, 137th Infantry Company I.

Along with several other companies of American troops, we were making our way through dense woods, towards the Rhine River in the German Rhineland. Our objective was to reach and take the town of Ossenberg, where a factory was producing gunpowder and other products for use in the war.

For hours we had pressed through an unrelenting thicket. Shortly after midday word was passed that there was a clearing ahead. At last, we thought, the going would be easier. But then we approached a large stone house, behind which huddled a handful of wounded, bleeding soldiers who had tried to cross the clearing and failed.

Before us stretched at least 200 yards of open ground, bordered on the far side by more thick woods. As the first of us appeared on the edge of the clearing there was an angry rat-tat-tat and a ferocious volley of bullets sent soil spinning as far as we could see. Three nests of German machine guns, spaced 50 yards apart and protected by the crest of a small hill to the left, were firing across the field. As we got our bearings it was determined that the machine guns were so well placed that our weapons couldn't reach them.

To cross that field meant suicide. Yet, we had no choice. The Germans had blockaded every other route into the town. In order to move on and secure a victory, we had to move forward.

---

48 E. M. Bounds. *The Best of E. M. Bounds on Prayer* (Grand Rapids, Michigan: Baker Book House; 1981), 75.

I slumped against a tree, appalled at the grim situation. I thought of home, of my wife and my 5-month-old son. I had kissed him good-bye just after he was born. I thought that I might never see my family again, and the possibility was overwhelming.

I dropped to my knees. "God," I pleaded desperately, "You've got to do something. Please do something."

Moments later the order was given to advance. Grasping my M-1 rifle, I go to my feet and started forward. After reaching the edge of the clearing I took a deep breath. But just before I stepped out from cover, I glanced to the left.

I stopped and stared in amazement. A white cloud – a long fluffy white cloud – had appeared out of nowhere. It dropped from over the trees and covered the area. The Germans' line of fire was obscured by the thick foggy mist.

All of us bolted into the clearing and raced for our lives. The only sounds were of combat boots thudding against the soft earth as men dashed into the clearing, scrambling to reach the safety of the other side before the mist lifted. With each step the woods opposite came closer and closer. I was almost across! My pulse pounding in my ears, I lunged into the thicket and threw myself behind a tree.

I turned and watched as other soldiers following me dove frantically into the woods, some carrying and dragging the wounded. This has to be God's doing, I thought. The instant the last man reached safety, the cloud vanished! The day was again bright and clear.

The enemy, apparently thinking we were still pinned down behind the stone house on the other side, must have radioed their artillery. Minutes later the building was blown to bits but our company was safe and we quickly moved on.

We reached Ossenberg and went on to secure more areas for the Allies. But the image of that cloud was never far from my mind. I had seen the sort of smoke screens that were sometimes set off to obscure troop activity in such situations. That cloud had been different. It had appeared out of nowhere and saved our lives.

Two weeks later, as we bivouacked in eastern Germany, a letter arrived from my mother back in Dallas.

I tore open the envelope eagerly. The letter contained words that sent a shiver down my spine. "You remember Mrs. Tankersly from our church?" my mother wrote.

Who could forget her? I smiled. Everybody called Mrs. Tankersly the prayer warrior.

"Well," continued Mom, "Mrs. Tankersly telephoned me one morning from the defense plant where she works. She said the Lord had awakened her the night before at one o' clock and told her, 'Spencer January is in terrible trouble. Get up now and pray for him!"

My mother went on to explain that Mrs. Tankersly had interceded for me in prayer until six o' clock the next morning, when she had to go to her job. "She told me the last thing she prayed before getting off her knees was this "Lord, whatever danger Spencer is in, just cover him with a cloud!"

I sat there for a long time holding the letter in my trembling hand. My mind raced, quickly calculating. Yes, the hours Mrs. Tankersly was praying would indeed have corresponded to the time we were approaching the clearing. With a seven-hour time difference, her prayer for a cloud would have been uttered at one o'clock, the exact time Company I was getting ready to cross the clearing.

From that moment on, I intensified my prayer life. For the past 52 years I have gotten up early every morning to pray for others. I am convinced there is no substitute for the power of prayer and its ability to comfort and sustain others, even those facing the valley of the shadow of death.[49]

There is power through persistent prayer, prayer that is beyond us, bigger than us, prayer by pure-hearted, but less than perfect saintly people, passionate and intense prayer, prayer that we do not even understand, prayer that stretches our perspective of things and calls us into the mysterious ways of God.

---

49 The personal testimony of Spencer January.

Discussion Questions

1. Are we surprised when God answers prayer? Do we expect answers – or, as in Acts 3, do answers disturb us?

2. Have we, like the apostles, allowed an imbalance with inadequate time for prayer? Do we expect our pastor(s) to pray? Or, perform his ministerial tasks (wait on tables)?

3. In the example of Herod, God directly intervened and judged the king. Should we pray for judgement on wicked leaders?

4. Peter was delivered by angelic intervention. Do such things happen today?

5. Must of our praying is narrow and self-interested. Talk about prayer and mission. How many of the illustrations of prayer interactions in this chapter are related to mission?

Nothing would turn the nation back to God so surely and so quickly as a Church that prayed and prevailed.

The world will never believe in a religion in which there is no supernatural power.

A rationalized faith, a socialized Church and a moralized gospel may gain applause, but they awaken no conviction and win no converts.

Samuel Chadwick

If the word "pray" is used 313 times in the Word of God, it must be an imperative—that of expressing a command in a forceful and confident way. Doug Small has taken praying to a higher level of influence with the Schools of Prayer. To really experience change, involve your church with multiple churches in your area for greater impact of the prayer implementation. Prayer changes people and people change the world! Acts 4:31 ... "And when they had prayed, the place was shaken!"

Dr. Timothy M. Hill, General Overseer
Church of God

I first met Doug Small at a Heart-Cry for Revival conference. I immediately began to see his heart and passion for prayer and unity. Having shared speaking times with him at a Revival forum and seeing his strategy for praying for a city, was revolutionary. His ability to speak across denominational lines to the things that should unite it rather than the secondary things that can divide us, was a great encouragement to me.

Pastor Michael Catt, Lead Pastor
Sherwood Baptist, Albany, GA

Doug Small brings an engaging, energetic, and Holy Spirit sensitive voice to the body of Christ. The Holy Spirit is using him to connect Christians from across denominational lines and bring us back to a fresh understanding of our unity in Christ. Doug's passion for righteousness stirs my heart to prayer for our nation and world.

Dr. Doug Beacham, General Superintendent
International Pentecostal Holiness Church

Doug Small is a highly-respected national prayer leader with a passion for bringing a fresh air of prayer to the local church. He equips through a powerful mix of biblical and practical teaching with strategic and prophetic insights. More than a seminar of notes and quotes, Doug creates a transformative spiritual experience for any church eager to become prayer-driven for the Gospel of Jesus Christ.

Phil Miglioratti,
Mission America Coalition, National Facilitator

When our organization wanted someone who understood how to foster a culture of powerful prayer, we turned to Doug Small. He brought Biblical, Christ-exalting messages coupled with a winsome spirit and presentation. If you long to ignite lasting impact in your congregation, Doug is a spiritual flame-starter!

Byron Paulus, President,
Life Action Ministries

JOIN THE
MOVEMENT

A network of local prayer leaders who are on a journey to bring prayer to the heart of all they do.

- Be encouraged
- Challenged
- Inspired and
- Resourced

REGISTER FOR FREE

OR BECOME A PREMIUM MEMBER FOR EVEN MORE VALUE!

WWW.PROJECTPRAY.ORG

AS PART OF THE MOVEMENT

BECOME A

Certified Prayer Trainer

Join others who affirm the goals of the Praying Church Movement and facilitate groups of prayer leaders from various churches to create an on-going forum for learning, training and encouragement.

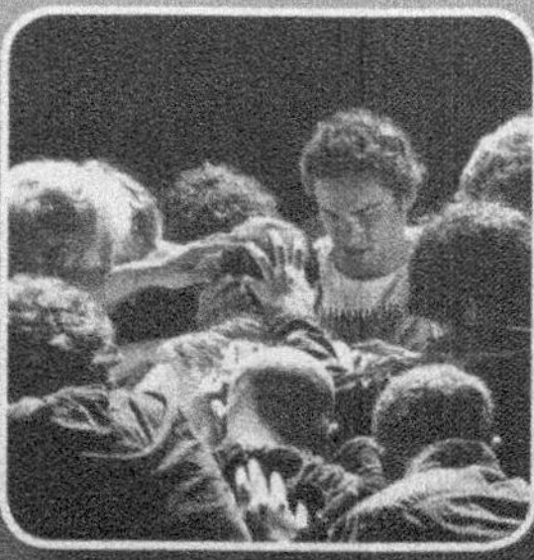

- Prayer Training
- Tool-time – Fresh Resources
- Talk-it-over/Take-it-home Application
- Quarterly Continuing Education

Host a
School of Prayer with P. Douglas Small

Schools of Prayer are seminars structured around learning and experiencing prayer.

Topics include:

- Enriching Your Personal Prayer Life
- Praying Through the Tabernacle
- Prayer the Heartbeat of the Church
- Heaven is a Courtroom
- Theology and Philosophy for Prayer Ministry
- Organizing Intercessors
- Entertaining God
- The Critical Strategic Uncomfortable Middle

www.projectpray.org
855-84-ALIVE